W9-DCZ-898

THE SHAKESPEARE LIBRARY.
GENERAL EDITOR PROFESSOR
I. GOLLANCZ, LITT.D.

THE · SHAKESPEARE · CLASSICS
B·McM·

THE TAMING OF A SHREW

A

Pleaſant Conceited

Hiſtorie, called The taming of a Shrew.

As it was ſundrie times acted by the *Right honorable the Earle of* Pembrook his ſeruants.

Imprinred at London by P. S. and are to be ſold by Cuthbert Burbie, at his ſhop at the Royall Exchange.

1596.

Title of the Edition of 1596, from a copy in the British Museum.

‘THE TAMING OF A SHREW’ BEING THE ORIGINAL OF SHAKESPEARE’S ‘TAMING OF THE SHREW’ EDITED BY F. S. BOAS, M.A.

NEW YORK
DUFFIELD AND COMPANY
LONDON: CHATTO & WINDUS
1908

READ THE BOOK OF TAMING A SHREW, WHICH HATH MADE A NUMBER OF US SO PERFECT, THAT NOW EVERY ONE CAN RULE A SHREW IN OUR COUNTRY, SAVE HE THAT HATH HER.

SIR JOHN HARINGTON (1596).

INTRODUCTION

EDITIONS OF THE PLAY

Early Editions.—There are three early editions of *The Taming of a Shrew.* The first was entered in the Stationers' Registers on 2nd May, 1594, to Peter Short, as "A plesant Conceyted historie called the Tamyinge of a Shrowe." It appeared in the same year in a quarto edition, with the following title: *A Pleasant Conceited Historie, called The taming of a Shrew. As it was sundry times acted by the Right honorable the Earle of Pembrook his servants. Printed at London by Peter Short and are to be sold by Cutbert Burbie, at his shop at the Royall Exchange,* 1594. The only surviving copy of this edition, as far as is known, is that in the Duke of Devonshire's library at Chatsworth. Except that it frequently confuses verse and prose, the text appears to be in the main accurate. The second edition, which was not entered on the Register, appeared in 1596. It was, like the first, printed by Short and sold by Burbie. Copies are preserved in the British Museum and in the Earl of Ellesmere's collection at Bridgewater House. This edition differs from its predecessor in comparatively few points, and these not of much significance. The title-page is reproduced as frontispiece to the present volume.

The third edition was published in 1607, but the copyright had now changed hands. *The taming of a Shrewe*, with *Romeo and Juliett* and *Loves Labour Loste* are entered in the Stationers' Registers on 22nd January, 1606/7 to "Master Linge by direccon of A Court and with consent of Master Burby under his handwrytinge." The quarto accordingly appeared with the imprint, "Printed at London by V. S. for Nicholas Ling, and are to be sold at his shop in Saint Dunstons Church-yard in Fleet street. 1607."[1] Copies of it are preserved at Chatsworth, and in the Malone Collection in the Bodleian Library. This edition, following its predecessor after an interval of eleven years, differs from it and the first quarto in a number of readings. In some points, especially the use of the plural verb instead of a singular before two nominatives, it shows a more modern tendency than the editions of 1594 or 1596. But the variants rarely extend to more than a few words, and they are superficial in character. The play in all essentials preserves the same text in the three original editions.

Later Reprints.—The publication of *The Taming of the Shrew* in the Shakespearean First Folio of 1623, in the quarto edition of 1631, and in the later Folios, doubtless checked any demand for the older play. Thus it had to wait for more than one hundred and seventy years after the publication of the quarto of 1607 before it was reprinted.

[1] In the same year Ling transferred his rights in the play to John Smethwick, who never published it, but brought out a quarto of *The Taming of the Shrew* in 1631.

In 1779 J. Nichols included it in his edition of *Six Old Plays* which had been used as sources by Shakespeare, and which he published at George Steevens' suggestion. It was printed, though not quite accurately, and without notes of any kind, from the quarto of 1607, which was the only text known to Steevens.

No further impression appeared till 1844, when Thomas Amyot brought out an edition for the Shakespeare Society. In this he reproduced the text of the first quarto, with footnotes containing the variants in the issues of 1596 and 1607. Though these variants were not exhaustive, Amyot's edition was a valuable piece of work. It was reproduced in Mr. W. C. Hazlitt's edition of Collier's *Shakespeare's Library*, Part II., Vol. ii. (1875).

A facsimile of the 1594 quarto was made by Mr. E. W. Ashbee in 1876, and another by photo-lithography by Mr. C. Praetorius in 1886. The facsimile of 1886 has interesting "Forewords" by Dr. F. J. Furnivall, who further arranged the play in nineteen Scenes, preceded by an Induction in two Scenes, and indicated the corresponding Acts and Scenes of the Shakespearean play. Lines containing words "that have been more or less taken up into *The Shrew*" were specially marked and numbered.

Text and Arrangement of this Edition.—The text of the present edition is based on that of the quarto of 1594. As the unique original was not available for collation, I have made use of the facsimile of Mr. Praetorius. In a few cases I have adopted the reading of the later quartos. These are inserted in square brackets. All other variants in these quartos, of which I collated the British Museum and Bodleian copies respectively, are recorded in the Textual Notes, which are fuller than in any previous edition. I have (not without some regret) modernised the spelling of the text, in accordance with the general scheme of the *Shakespeare Classics* Series. But as in the Textual Notes I have given from the quarto of 1594 every original spelling which seemed worthy of record, I hope that little will be lost to those who cling to Elizabethan orthography in an Elizabethan play.

There is one other respect in which the text in this edition differs from that of the quartos or of the later reprints. I have printed as prose a number of passages which appear in earlier editions in doggerel verse form, and in a few cases I have restored lines printed as prose to what I believe to have been their original metrical arrangement. It is impossible to attain to perfect certainty in such transpositions. Allowances have to be made for faulty readings in the text, and for changes of pronunciation. I have therefore retained the verse arrangement of the quartos in some doubtful cases, and in every instance of change the original form is given in the Textual Notes. But it seemed to me the duty of a modern editor, who was not merely reprinting the play in facsimile, to attempt to the best of his ability to correct the effects of the notorious carelessness of Elizabethan printers in this particular matter.

I have also for the first time divided the play into Acts, with subdivisions into Scenes. Any such arrangement must be regarded as tentative, for the comments of Sly and the other watchers of what is technically a play within a play do not (like those of Andrea's Ghost and Revenge in *The Spanish Tragedy*) always indicate the close of an Act. At one or two of the chief turning-points in the action of the plot Sly keeps silence, and on the other hand one of his interventions (IV. ii. 45-53) is obviously in the middle of a Scene.

But the following arrangement, which has been adopted in this edition, will, I believe, be found to correspond in the main with the natural articulation of the plot. First comes the Induction, divided into two Scenes, in the former of which Sly is discovered by the hunting lord in front of the alehouse, and in the second is cheated into the belief that he is the master of the mansion to which he has been transported in his drunken sleep. The first Act of the play proper extends to line 323, when the stage is for the first time left empty, except for Sly and the lord (with his followers), who here intervene with a few lines of dialogue. The second Act, divided into two Scenes, ends with the departure of Ferando and Kate, immediately after their wedding, to the former's country house, leaving the other guests to eat the marriage dinner that Alfonso had prepared. The third Act includes the episodes at Ferando's house, and ends with the announcement of the immediate marriage of Aurelius and Philema, and of Polidor and Emelia, which draws from Sly a brief query. In the fourth Act the chief figure is the Duke of Sestos, who discloses the trick that Aurelius has played on Alfonso; the Act ends with his departure from Athens, and is followed by the episode of the lord ordering his servants to carry back the sleeping Sly to the place where he had been found. The fifth Act contains the final test of the obedience of the three brides to their respective husbands, while the closing dialogue between Sly and the Tapster forms the Epilogue to the whole work.

The headings of Acts and Scenes, including the indication in each case of the locality where the action takes place, are distinguished from the original stage directions by square brackets. Other slight deviations from the stage directions of the quartos are recorded in the Textual Notes.

HISTORY OF THE STORIES IN THE PLAY

The Induction.—The story of the low-born sleeper tricked into the belief that he is a personage of high estate, is very ancient, and forms a well-known episode in the *Arabian Nights*. It has been conjectured that it was told to Philip the Good, Duke of Burgundy, in the middle of the fifteenth century, by one of the Eastern embassies that visited his court, and that he was thus inspired to imitate the jest of Haroun Alraschid. However this may be, Heuterus in his Latin chronicle *De Rebus Burgundicis* (1584)[1] relates from a

[1] Quoted by Warton in *History of English Poetry*, Vol. iii., pp. 294-5. He refers to Book IV., p. 150, of the 1584 edition of *De Rebus Burgundicis*.

letter of Ludovicus Vives an anecdote of how the Duke wandering one night with some friends came upon a ragged fellow lying in a drunken stupor, and played exactly the same trick upon him as the nobleman does on Sly in *The Taming of a Shrew.* It is curious that among the entertainments provided for the mock-Duke, plays are expressly mentioned (*exhibitæ sunt fabulæ*). A French version of the story was included by Simon Goulart in his *Thrésor d'histoires admirables et mémorables* (probably 1606), which was translated by Edward Grimeston in 1607. Another slighter version is given by Burton in his *Anatomy of Melancholy*, Part II., Sec. ii., Mem. 4 (1621). It was probably about the same date that the story appeared in its most elaborate form, with the title *The Waking Man's Dreame.* It is preserved in a fragment, paged 59-67, of a work which has otherwise disappeared, and is headed "The Fifth Event," being evidently one of a series of tales. This fragment was discovered by Mr. H. G. Norton, who reprinted it in Vol. ii. of the Shakespeare Society's Papers (1845). He thought that the volume of which it formed part was a reprint of a black-letter collection of short comic stories in prose issued by Richard Edwardes, the dramatist, in 1570. No copy of this black-letter work now exists, but Warton in his *History of English Poetry*, III., 292-4, states he had seen one among the books of William Collins of Chichester, and that it contained the story of the Induction. Norton's conjecture is, however, very doubtful. I agree with Mr. Warwick Bond (Introduction to Arden edition of the *Taming of the Shrew*, pp. xlviii.-ix.) that *The Waking Man's Dreame*, "with the extension of the tale to include subsequent relations between the Duke and his butt, not given in Heuterus," has all the air of being "a later development" instead of an early version of the story. It is probably founded on the Goulart-Grimeston narrative. Mr. Bond has noticed that the anonymous author, like Grimeston, refers to Seneca. A still closer coincidence is that in both versions the mock-Duke is represented as drinking a particular wine, "Ipocras," at the banquet to which he is entertained.[1] There are other minor verbal parallelisms, and it is noticeable that the author of *The Waking Man's Dreame* excuses himself for including among his "Events" one "published by any other writer," on the ground that its "repetition will neither be unfruitfull nor unpleasing."

Sir Richard Barckley, in his *Discourse of the Felicitie of Man* (1598), had given an earlier English version of the story than

[1] It is also noticeable that the writer of *The Waking Man's Dreame* agrees with Goulart-Grimeston in laying the scene of the episode in Brussels. Heuterus, who introduces it incidentally in his final observations upon Philip the Good's character and rule, assigns it to Brughes, but does not particularise the time of the incident. Warton, however, in quoting his account, speaks of the episode as "having happened at the marriage of Duke Philip—about the year 1440." He apparently refers to the Duke's third marriage, with Isabella of Portugal, which took place on 10th January, 1430, at Bruges. Burton places the incident at Bruges on the occasion of this marriage (though he mistakenly calls the bride Eleonora) and states that as Philip was deprived of other amusements by the wintry weather, he used in the evening to walk disguised about the town.

Grimeston. He did not assign it, however, to the reign of Philip of Burgundy, but speaks of it as a "pretie experiment practised by the Emperour *Charles* the fift upon a drunkard," and lays the scene in Ghent. Whatever may be the exact historical foundation for these various narratives, it is plain from its frequent repetition that the story had caught hold of men's imaginations in the Elizabethan age, and that the author of *The Taming of a Shrew* was well advised in putting it into dramatic form. But he cannot have drawn upon any of the extant versions, which were all later than the play except the Latin narrative of Heuterus, which is most unlikely to have been known to him.[1]

The Shrew Story.—The story of the main plot, dealing, as it does, with an eternal problem in the relation of the sexes, is by its very nature of immemorial antiquity, and is found, in different forms, in the literature of all countries. It is, therefore, only necessary to allude here to such versions of the theme as are specifically akin to the treatment of it in the present play. Of these the most remarkable is a Danish story included in a collection made by Grundtvig, and summarised by Köhler in *Shakespeare Jahrbuch*, Vol. III., 397-401 (1868). It tells of three sisters, Karen, Maren, and Mette, of whom the third is the most shrewish, and the last to find a husband. Her bridegroom, like Ferando, appears at the ceremony on the wedding-day late and unsuitably dressed. He is mounted on an old

1 The versions of the story given by Heuterus, Goulart-Grimeston, Barckley, and in *The Waking Man's Dreame* are reprinted in *Appendix II*.

horse, and has a dog at his side, and immediately after the marriage he carries off his bride, as Ferando does Kate, to his own home in spite of her father's remonstrances. The incidents that follow have no parallel in the play. On the journey the bridegroom, as a lesson to his wife, shoots his dog, and afterwards his horse, for disobedience to his orders. He then gathers a switch, bends the ends together, and tells Mette to keep it till he asks for it. She becomes an exemplary wife, and after a long period he proposes that they should visit her parents. From this point the resemblances between the story and the play reappear. Twice they start and twice they return because her docility is not equal to accepting her husband's assertions that storks are ravens and a flock of sheep are wolves. On the third occasion, however, she assents to fowls being called crows, and thus she is allowed to return to her former home, where her sisters with their husbands have preceded her. The father offers a jug full of money to the son-in-law with the most obedient wife. The two other sisters prove recalcitrant even when personally summoned by their husbands. But Mette, when called much more peremptorily, comes at once to know her husband's will. He asks for the switch he had given her, and when she brings it, he points the moral to the husbands of Karen and Maren in the words: "I bent the wand when it was green; you should have done so too."

Ticknor, in his *History of Spanish Literature* (1842), Vol. I., 77, drew attention to a resemblance between the Taming of the Shrew story and the forty-fourth story in *El Conde*

Lucanor, a collection of fifty tales by Don Juan Manuel, nephew of Alfonso the Wise, who lived from 1282 to 1347. The first edition was published at Madrid in 1575. In this tale a young Moor marries the daughter of a neighbour, who has the reputation of being such a virago that her father declares that her husband will soon die, or, at least, find death preferable to life. On the evening of the wedding-day the young couple sit down to supper alone. The husband kills in succession his dog, cat, and horse because they do not carry out his order to bring him water to wash his hands, and cries out that "any one living who dares to disobey me shall not escape my vengeance." When he turns to his wife, and bids her bring the water, she is too terrified to disobey. And she afterwards meekly carries out his further orders, to get up and prevent him from being disturbed in his sleep, and to prepare a meal for him when he should wake. In the morning the relatives, who have approached the room, are amazed, when the bride bids them be silent, lest her husband should kill them and her, and they much esteem the young man. "And from that time forward his wife became tractable and complaisant, so that they led a very happy life."[1]

Ticknor somewhat exaggerated the likeness between this story and the plot of *A Shrew*. The resemblance consists in the husband's successful assertion of his authority immediately after the marriage ceremony, but the details are entirely

[1] The story is told fully in the first English translation of *El Conde Lucanor*, by Dr. James York, 1848, pp. 200-6.

different, and the episode of the bridegroom killing his animals for their disobedience is akin to that part of the Danish folk-tale which diverges most from the plot of *A Shrew*.

But, curiously enough, there is another tale in *El Conde Lucanor*, the fifth in the collection, which bears a close resemblance to incidents in Acts III. v. and IV. i. of the present play. The wife of Don Alvar Fañez, amazes his nephew, who is their guest, by endorsing her husband's statements when he calls a herd of cows mares, and *vice-versa*. The nephew thinks that he must have lost his senses, and is confirmed in this when Don Alvar declares that a river runs up to its source, and is again supported by his wife. But Don Alvar afterwards explains to the nephew that his wife never contradicts him, because she believes that he always judges and acts for the best, and that therefore he can give her an amount of liberty which the nephew had blamed as excessive. The likeness, as Mr. Warwick Bond has pointed out, between the *Shrew* story and Straparola's *Piacevoli Notti*, VIII., 2 (1553), where the attitude of two sisters to their husbands is sharply contrasted, is not close enough to need detailed comment. From about the same period, according to Collier, dates the English piece of narrative verse, *A Merry Jest of a Shrewd and Curst Wife Lapped in Morel's Skin*. Laneham's *Letter* (1575) gives evidence of its popularity by mentioning it as a story which Captain Cox had "at hiz fingers endz." But if, as is probable, the author of *The Taming of a Shrew* knew this coarsely realistic account of a termagant wife being whipped and wrapped in the salted hide of her husband's horse, he showed his artistic perception by turning his back upon such crude and ugly methods of curing a rebellious bride. Though Ferando's fashion of taming Kate is drastic according to modern ideas, it is to be noted that he never lifts a finger against her, and one of the cardinal merits of the play is that it breaks with the popular stage-tradition, illustrated in such a work as *Tom Tiler*, that the cudgel is the only medicine for a shrew.

The Underplot.—The courtship of the younger sisters of Kate by Aurelius and Polidor is entirely in the vein of sixteenth century Italian comedy. It is, in fact, difficult to resist the conclusion formed independently by Prof. Tolman (*Publications of the Modern Language Association of America*, Vol. V., 4) and Mr. Warwick Bond (*Introduction to the Taming of the Shrew*, pp. xliii.-iv.), that the author of *The Taming of a Shrew*, though less indebted than Shakespeare to Gascoigne's *Supposes* (1566), the English version of Ariosto's *I Suppositi* (1509), drew from it certain features of the underplot. The arrival of Aurelius in a strange city, and his sudden passion for Philema; his command to his servant Valeria to impersonate him while he woos his mistress in disguise; the suborning of Phylotus to play the part of father to Aurelius, and to promise a handsome marriage settlement; the unexpected arrival on the scene of the lover's real father, who exposes the imposture; Aurelius' confession, followed by forgiveness and a general reconciliation—all these, though names[1] and other details are changed, have

[1] See Appendix III., A.

their exact parallel in *Supposes*. For this part of the play, therefore, we seem to be able to point to a direct source; elsewhere, as appears above, we cannot do more than trace analogies.

DATE OF THE PLAY

The exact date of the play is uncertain, though it must fall within somewhat narrow limits. The entry in the Stationers' Register fixes the beginning of May, 1594, as the latest period for the composition of the work, and it is probably to be assigned to a date several years previous. The statement on the title-page of the first edition that it had been performed "sundry times" by the Earl of Pembroke's servants, does not help us much, partly because of the uncertainty when Pembroke's company was formed. The first definite allusion to them, as Mr. Greg shows (*Henslowe's Diary*, Part II., p. 104) is on 11th March, 1593, in *The Acts of the Privy Council*, when a warrant was issued to Sir Thomas Heneage to pay them for two plays acted at Court on the preceding 27th December and 6th January. We next hear of them in a letter of Henslowe to Alleyn, in September, 1593, in which he reports that "they are ar all at home and hausse ben this v or sixe weackes for they cane not save their carges wth travell as I heare & weare fayne to pane ther parell for ther carge." They appear, as Mr. Greg adds, not only to have had to pawn their wardrobe, but to part with some of their plays, either to booksellers or to rival companies. They seem to have disposed of *The Taming of a Shrew* in both ways, for, as already stated, it was licensed for publication in May, 1594, and in June of the same year, it was acted by the Lord Chamberlain's and the Lord Admiral's men at Newington.

How long Pembroke's company had been in existence before its first Court performance on 27th December, 1902, is uncertain. Mr. Fleay's statement that they "are first heard of in London in 1589" (*Chronicle History of the London Stage*, p. 87) is merely a conjecture, based upon a passage in Nash's Preface to Greene's *Menaphon*. Nor do we know when they acquired *The Taming of a Shrew*. But the fact that the author quotes largely from Marlowe's *Tamburlaine* and *Dr. Faustus*, acted in all probability in 1588 and 1589, while he does not draw upon his later plays, makes it probable that *The Taming of a Shrew* was produced about 1590 or not long afterwards.[1]

[1] One simile, indeed, in Act II., i., 149-50, "Whiter than . . . icy hair that grows on Boreas' chin," was evidently in Greene's mind when he wrote in *Menaphon* (1589) of the ewe "whose fleece was as white as the haires that grow on father *Boreas* chinne, or as the dangling deaw-lap of the silver Bull," while Nash in his Preface to Greene's novel similarly refers to the vainglorious tragedians who "get Boreas by the beard, and the heavenlie bull by the deaw-lap." If Greene and Nash were here alluding to *The Taming of a Shrew*, the date of the play would necessarily be before 1589, but the author may well have borrowed the simile, which occurs in a speech pieced together mainly from fragments of Marlowe (*cf.* Appendix I. (10), (11), and (12)), from an older play, now lost. This is the more probable, as both Greene and Nash combine the reference to Boreas' chin with that to the dewlap of the Bull, to which there is nothing corresponding in *The Taming of a Shrew*.

GENERAL CHARACTERISTICS OF THE PLAY

Some Preliminary Points.—Though the text of the play, as has been already stated, appears in the main to have been satisfactorily presented in the quartos, there are some peculiar points which give colour to the view that the piece was printed from an acting version. Thus the principal player in the Induction is called Sander, which is the name of Ferando's man in the comedy itself. It looks as if the same actor played both parts, and perhaps gave his own name to them. This is, however, not the only case of the reduplication of names. The second player in the Induction is called Tom (i. 83). One of the lord's serving men is also Tom, and his fellow is Will (ii. 18), and the same names are given to two of Ferando's servants at his country house. The lord in the Induction tells Sly to call him Simon, and it is curious that after Act I. i. 21, the quartos mention a "Simon" as entering with Alfonso and his daughters, though there is no further hint of such a personage in the play.

Alfonso's opening words in the above passage, where he bids his daughters hie them "to the church," are singularly abrupt, and look as if they were suggested by something in the unknown source of the play. There is, too, a striking inconsistancy between Act I. i. 86-92 and ll. 276-8 of the same Scene. In the earlier passage Aurelius forthwith arranges that to win Philema he will disguise himself as "a merchant's son of Sestos," while his servant Valeria personates him as the prince. But in ll. 276-8 he suddenly bids Valeria, "as erst we did devise," assume the rôle of a music-master to Kate, and it is not till Act III. ii. that the original plan is carried out.

Combination of Plots in the Play.—We have therefore to remember in any general estimate of the merits of the play, that some of its details seem to have been faultily transmitted, or need a knowledge of its source for their interpretation. But its main characteristics stand out clearly, and entitle it to an honourable place in Elizabethan dramatic history, even if it had never been reshaped by Shakespeare into the form with which all the world is familiar. Its dominant merit is that it unites in one framework three plots of interesting and very diverse types. The dizzying elevation of Sly for a few hours from the gutter to the palace appeals to the eternal instinct which delights in the sudden revolution of human fortunes, even though, as in this case, it is but a mockery as unsubstantial as a dream. The taming of Kate by a bridegroom as stubborn and as self-willed as herself, and even more fertile in resource, is an episode in the ever fascinating Protean duel of the sexes. The courtship of the two younger sisters of the shrew by two wooers who are supposed to be profiting in the "public schools" of Athens, and one of whom is a duke's son in disguise, not only contains the element of sentimental love-making which corrects the acid flavour of the main plot, but ministers to the delight in mistaken identity so characteristic of the Elizabethan age, and not extinct in our own.

Moreover, in the management of these stories and in their combination, the author shows a true instinct for dramatic technique. He is comparatively free from the besetting sin of so many Elizabethan playwrights of elaborating single scenes without regard to the perspective and proportion of the work as a whole. Though the style is in parts over-rhetorical, there is scarcely a speech or incident which is not germane to the development of the plot. It is in this skilfully economic use of his materials that the anonymous dramatist's main power lies.

The connection of the Sly story with the plots of the main play is cleverly developed in the incidental snatches of dialogue between the drunkard and the lord. Thus at the end of Act I. Sly's query, "when will the fool come again?" is an all-sufficient revelation of his theatrical taste, and his immediate call for "some more drink" shows that no higher form of entertainment can stifle his grosser appetites. A still more masterly stroke is found in Act IV. ii. 45 ff, when the Duke of Sestos orders Valeria and Phylotus to prison, and Sly, who has doubtless been a gaol-bird once and again, bursts in excitedly, "I say we'll have no sending to prison." And when in the Epilogue Sly awakens out of his "dream" to the harsh realities of life, he foreshadows a practical application of his night's experiences in the threat to "tame" his wife "and if she anger" him.

In the play proper the plots of the taming of Kate and the courtship of her younger sisters move for the most part on parallel lines. But at various points the threads of the two actions are deftly enough interwoven. The success of Aurelius and Polidor in their love-suits is made dependent from the first upon the course of Ferando's wooing, and Valeria undertakes the duties of Kate's music-master that her sisters may "steal abroad," while she is busy with her lessons on the lute (I. i. 288 ff). Later in the play the marriage of the younger sisters provides a reason for the return of Kate and her husband from the country to her father's house, and their encounter on the way with the Duke of Sestos, who has come in quest of his son, gives Ferando the opportunity of putting his wife's novel docility to an overwhelming test. And in the last Act the wager between the husbands upon their respective brides' obedience, with its astounding result, gathers up the threads of the two plots in an unforeseen and effective way.

Character-drawing.—It is in plot rather in character-drawing that the author's strength lies. The most striking portrait is that of Sly, etched with bold, hard-bitten strokes. He is a type, taken doubtless from the life, of an irredeemable sluggard and sot, a mere creature of appetites, but with a racy tongue and a cool self-possession which make him equally at ease in the alehouse or the castle. With the full-length portraits of Ferando and Kate the dramatist's success is less complete. Both are drawn with spirit and vigour, and the scenes between them, especially in Ferando's country house, have a boisterous vitality which is, within limits, thoroughly effective. We recognise that two strong natures are fighting for mastery, and from the first we see that Ferando, by virtue of the heavier metal of his sex, is bound to win the day! But all finer touches, to give subtlety and relief to either figure, are absent. There is no hint in Ferando of an underlying tenderness towards the woman whose will must be broken for her own happiness as well as his own. He embarks on his wooing because her father has promised him six thousand crowns if he can win her hand, and he carries through his enterprise in the spirit of an adventurer who will use any means to gain his end. And Kate's transformation from the "devilish scold" of Act I. to the docile wife of Act V. is crudely motived, and is too largely due to physical ill-treatment and humiliation. When in the midst of an outburst against Ferando she abruptly interjects the aside (I. i. 169-71)—

> "But yet I will consent and marry him,
> For I methinks have lived too long a maid,
> And match him, too, or else his manhood's good"—

we feel that the playwright, in spite of his genuine gifts, is quite unequal to the analysis of the intricate workings of the feminine heart. And the theological argument upon which she finally bases the duty of wives to obey their husbands (V. i. 116 ff.) sounds absurdly inappropriate on the lips of one who has been tamed, not by reasoning, but by the most rough and ready practical methods.

The racy vigour which is the playwright's chief gift in character-drawing, appears also in rougher form in the figures of Sander and Polidor's boy. Sander is a thoroughly entertaining specimen of the swaggering, familiar, sharp-tongued, but withal good-humoured serving-man, who enters with gusto into his master's plans for "taming" his bride. With his airs and graces as "good Master Sander," his condescending manner to the boy, his weakness for grandiloquent phrases, and his aspirations after a family alliance with his master or his mistress (I. i. 219-22 and 524-7), he is a farcical anticipation of Malvolio, though there is not a drop of gall in his composition. Skilfully discriminated from Sander is the pert "hop of my thumb," the boy, who serves "young Polidor," quick with his tongue, and equally quick with his weapon when he thinks that his master's honour is in danger. Valeria on the other hand, the servant of Aurelius, has no individuality. He is merely a type borrowed from Italian comedy. This observation may, in fact, be made of all the personages in the sentimental underplot. Aurelius is in no wise distinguished from Polidor, nor Philema from Emelia. They are merely the stock lovers of the southern stage.

Style.—In style the play presents a remarkable medley of characteristics. It is written for the most part in simple, direct language—sometimes bald in its plainness, sometimes vivified by a racily vernacular phrase—which forms a thoroughly serviceable instrument for the playwright's purposes. And though he lacks the subtler elements of dramatic style, he has a noticeable gift of tersely humorous expression, which is a hall-mark of the born writer of comedy, and of which a few illustrations may be given.

Such is Ferando's greeting, at an early and unpropitious stage of his courtship, of Alfonso by the title of "father" (I. i. 177), with its cool assumption, in Kate's hearing, of his assured triumph. Again there is his capital retort, on the wedding-day, to Alfonso's query why he has come "thus basely attired":

> "Thus richly, father, you should have said;
> For when my wife and I am married once,
> She's such a shrew, if we should once fall out
> She'll pull my costly suits over mine ears,
> And therefore am I thus attired awhile."—(I. i. 444-9.)

And at the close of the play, when Ferando has won his wager upon Kate's obedience, how much genial wisdom is packed into Alfonso's words (V. i. 146-9):

> "And for to show thee how I am pleased in this,
> A hundred pounds I freely give thee more,
> Another dowry for another daughter,
> For she is not the same she was before."

The Marlowesque Passages.—But genuine and entertaining as are the writer's gifts of expression within their own limits, emotional and imaginative effects lay beyond his range. Here he fell back upon imitation of a greater than himself. Marlowe had just taken the London stage by storm, and the author of *The Taming of a Shrew* was evidently among his most enthusiastic devotees. The "high astounding terms," the melody and imagery of *Tamburlaine* and *Dr. Faustus* must have rung incessantly in his ear and brain, and he sought to match them to his own fustian muse. In Appendix I. to this volume a full list of the borrowed passages is given. A careful examination of them leads to several important conclusions. In the first place it is clear that though the borrowings are found chiefly in the underplot, they are by no means confined to it. Two of them occur in the Induction; several, including the most elaborate patchwork of quotations in the play, are put into the mouth of Ferando; another, the only prose bit "conveyed," is spoken by Ferando's man Sander. It is, therefore, in my opinion, a mistake to rest any argument against the unity of authorship of *A Shrew* upon the Marlowesque passages. They occur sporadically throughout the play in contexts of the most diverse kind, and they have every appearance of being the work, not of a collaborator, but of the original writer attempting at intervals to soar on borrowed plumes. But the effort is a lame one, and the more narrowly the borrowings are scrutinised in relation to their source, the less credit do they throw upon the conveyor. In some cases they convict him of curious ignorance of mythological lore, and in others they are grotesquely inappropriate to their new context. Thus in Induction, ii. 20-1, Pegasus is spoken of as the horse "that ran so swiftly o'er the Persian plains." The dramatist seems to have thought that because Pegasus is mentioned by Tamburlaine, and because in the next line garments of "Medean silke" are spoken of, that he was a Persian steed. Again, Marlowe makes the Soldan of Egypt swear appropriately by "Ibis holy name." The author of *A Shrew* not only puts a similar vow, with ridiculous incongruity, into the mouth of Ferando, but gives Ibis the fictitious attribute of a golden beak. Equally absurd on Ferando's lips is the reference (II. i. 131-2) to "the massy robe" of "the stately legate of the Persian king," which is compounded out of two allusions in *Tamburlaine*. And even if Ferando's high-flown Marlowesque address to Kate (II. i. 146-60) be looked upon merely as banter, nothing could be more grotesque than his comparison of her later, in a soliloquy, to (III. i. 50-1)—

> . . . "the Thracian horse Alcides tamed,
> That King Egeus fed with flesh of men."

Even on the lips of Tamburlaine, as addressed to the captive kings harnessed to his chariot, the comparison is incongruously extravagant; but in its new application it is a piece of sheer absurdity. Of Marlowe's many followers it may be safely said that none "learned his great language" in a more misguided way, or with more inept results, than the author of *The Taming of a Shrew*.

AUTHORSHIP OF THE PLAY

Marlowe, Kyd, and Greene.—Yet the modern commentator cannot entirely regret that the anonymous playwright borrowed, though to so little advantage, from his great contemporary. For not only, as I have sought to show elsewhere,[1] do the rifled passages help us in estimating

[1] See Appendix I.

the relative authority of the different texts of *Doctor Faustus*, but they form, from the negative point of view, important evidence in discussing the authorship of the play. I have already stated my opinion that only one hand is responsible for it. The idea of Marlowe himself having written it, which found favour with some critics, especially about the middle of the nineteenth century, has been increasingly abandoned, and is incredible to anyone who has considered fully the treatment of the passages from his works which appear in the play. From some points of view more might be urged on behalf of Kyd, to whom Mr. Fleay assigns the comedy in his *Biographical Chronicle*. The able plot-construction, the acidulated humour of some of the prose scenes, the device of a play within the play are all characteristic of the author of the *Spanish Tragedy*. But apart from the absence of other marked features of Kyd's style, it is most improbable that so original a dramatist, who himself was imitated and parodied incessantly, should have borrowed in so wholesale and tasteless a manner from his chief rival. This argument cannot be used with equal force against those who have assigned the play to Greene, who in *Alphonsus* and *Orlando Furioso* has obviously imitated the style and diction of Marlowe. But though, especially in the former work, he reproduced almost literally individual lines, he did not transfer connected passages from Marlowe's dramas, nor violate congruity so outrageously in his borrowings. Moreover Greene, if his extant plays are judged from a modern point of view, is weakest in plot construction, which is the chief excellence of *The Taming of a Shrew.* Moreover, the types of womanhood found in his plays are entirely unlike any of Alfonso's daughters, and I feel confident that had he written the country scenes, either of the Induction or of Acts III. and IV., he would have invested them with more of pastoral charm.

Shakespeare.—Finally we have to discuss the view that the present play is by none of the predecessors of Shakespeare, but is from the pen of the Stratford dramatist himself, and is his earlier draft of *The Taming of the Shrew.* This theory, though put forward from time to time with modifications of detail by critics both in England and Germany, has never gained wide acceptance, but has recently been revived by Mr. Courthope in its most undiluted form (*History of English Poetry*, Vol. iv., Ch. 4, and *Appendix*). Into the general argument by which Mr. Courthope seeks not only to defend the full authorship by Shakespeare of the three parts of *King Henry VI.* and *Titus Andronicus*, which are assigned to him in the First Folio, but also to establish his claim to be the "only begetter" of *The First Part of the Contention*, and *The True Tragedie*, and of *The Troublesome Raigne of King John* and *The Taming of a Shrew*—into this it is impossible to enter here at length. As far as the four plays not contained in the Folio are concerned, the claim rests mainly on the ground that, if it is rejected, Shakespeare is proved guilty of wholesale plagiarism in the works founded upon them. I agree with the critics who hold that modern views of literary paternity or copyright cannot be applied to Elizabethan plays, which were not written primarily for publication, and which as the property of one or other of the theatrical companies of the period were liable to be reshaped from time to time for stage purposes. Moreover, I am strongly of opinion that Shakespeare's debt to his predecessors and contemporaries in the matter of plots and scenic outlines is not yet recognised, partly owing to the disappearance of many early dramas, to be as large as actually was the case. And with regard to *The Taming of a Shrew*, whoever seeks to relieve Shakespeare of the charge of plagiarism by assigning it to him, is using a double-edged tool. There is no more open and unintelligent example of plagiarism in the whole range of Elizabethan drama than in the Marlowesque reproductions in the anonymous play. It is, in my opinion, impossible that Shakespeare, whose verbal quotations from Marlowe are confined to a very few individual lines, should have ever borrowed from him in this crude and indiscriminate fashion.

But apart from the Marlowesque passages altogether, internal evidence is, as far as I can judge, entirely against the attribution of the play to Shakespeare. Neither the versification, the language, nor the general technique is characteristic of him. Even in his earliest plays the blank verse is not so monotonously end-stopped as in *A Shrew*; there is more variety of rhythm and cadence. And the simple, homespun diction in which, as has been observed above, the comedy is for the most part written, is not

Shakespearean. Shakespeare's language is seldom simple, and is scarcely ever so except in the period of his matured, though not his latest, style. In the earliest stage of his career, when, *ex hypothesi*, *The Taming of a Shrew* would have been written, his diction differs from that in the play both for better and for worse. It is marred by conceits, verbal ingenuities and rhetoric, which are absent from *A Shrew*, but it is of closer texture, and is richer in imagery and in lyric grace.

In its general features also the play differs from Shakespeare's early comedies. I cannot believe that the Stratford dramatist, new come from Warwickshire scenes, could have penned the Induction or the episodes in Ferando's country house without introducing from the first the realistic details, the rural nomenclature of persons, animals, and places which give such life and pungency to the corresponding parts of *The Taming of the Shrew*. The older play seems to me to be the work of a town-bred dramatist who had no intimate knowledge of the country. And I do not think that even in his apprentice days Shakespeare could have taken over the figures of the underplot from Italian comedy without lending them some individualising touch. Aurelius and Polidor, Emelia and Philema are mere puppets—unlike the earliest and slightest Shakespearean character-sketches. Moreover, if Shakespeare in *The Taming of the Shrew* were revising an underplot some features of which he himself had already taken from *Supposes*, it is strange that he should have modelled his second version far more closely on the original than the first. And why should he have thought it worth while to shift the scene of the whole action from Athens to Padua, and to change the names of every character except Kate and Sly? As far as it is possible to prove anything by internal evidence, the arguments against the Shakespearean authorship of *The Taming of a Shrew* are, in my opinion, conclusive. Its *provenance*, like that of *Arden of Feversham*, is likely to remain one of the insoluble enigmas of Elizabethan dramatic history.

THE TAMING OF A SHREW AND THE TAMING OF THE SHREW

I do not propose to lengthen out this Introduction by discussing in detail the relation between the older comedy and *The Taming of a Shrew*. This is the function rather of an editor of the Shakespearean play, than of its predecessor. It has been often done, notably, of recent years, by Mr. Warwick Bond in his excellent Introduction to his edition of the play in the *Arden Shakespeare* (pp. xiv.-xxii.) I have myself discussed some aspects of the subject elsewhere (*Shakespeare and his Predecessors*, p. 172 ff.), and certain points have been already incidentally touched upon in this Introduction. Mr. Boswell-Stone's essay and parallel list of characters, reprinted in Appendix III., furnish the material for a comparison between the plots and *dramatis personæ* of *I Suppositi*, *A Shrew*, and *The Shrew*; and one of the objects of the present edition of the older comedy is to give students and readers generally facilities for further investigation on their own account.

It is therefore only necessary to say here that in *The Taming of the Shrew* Shakespeare gives one of the most remarkable examples of his unique faculty of transforming his materials, of vitalising and refining them, while largely preserving their substance. The general structure of the old play is retained, but it is enriched with new treasures of imagination, dramatic insight, and verbal music. In the Induction the capital sketch of Sly in the earlier comedy, as the type of a lazy, imperturbable, and free-spoken sot, is individualised into that masterpiece of low-life portraiture "Christopher Sly, old Sly's son, of Burton-heath," whose talk, with that of the lord's huntsmen and attendants, transports us into the rural atmosphere of the Midlands. Yet, whatever explanation may be given of it, the sudden dropping of the threads of the Sly story after Act I. Sc. i., is a blemish in the Shakespearean play, which in this respect is not so well rounded off as its predecessor.[1]

It is in the "taming" plot, with its three chief figures, Kate, Petruchio, and Grumio, that Shakespeare follows the older play most closely. The incidents, except in minor details, are parallel throughout, and in Act IV. i. and iii. portions of the original dialogue are incorporated with little transformation. But Petruchio's motives in wooing the

[1] For an interesting discussion of Shakespeare's possible motives for making this change, see Mr. Warwick Bond's edition of *The Taming of the Shrew*, pp. 32-3, note.

shrew are made more plausible and dignified than in the older play; it is clearer throughout that he is attracted by her charms, and that though his treatment is outwardly harsh, "all is done in reverent care of her." Both he and Kate are insensibly lifted to a higher plane than their prototypes in *A Shrew* by the greater refinement and flexibility of their speech, which rises in their softer moods to lyric sweetness. Grumio is perhaps not a more amusing rogue than Sander, but his humour is more mellow and rich.

The underplot goes through the fullest transformation, and the numerous critics who assign this part of *The Taming of the Shrew* to another hand than Shakespeare's are depriving him of the credit of a very ingenious and effective piece of adaptation. Without asserting the authenticity of every line or phrase, I see no reason to modify the view expressed at an earlier date, in *Shakespeare and his Predecessors*, that the underplot is substantially from the pen of the great dramatist. In its revised form it has much more animation and variety of interest than before. Instead of the two colourless younger sisters with their equally colourless lovers, there is one younger sister, Bianca, who makes a better foil to the shrew, and for whose hand there is an amusing rivalry between Lucentio and Hortensio (the Aurelius and Polidor of *A Shrew*) and the foolish greybeard Gremio, imported from *Supposes*. The development of the intrigue, with its complex series of impersonations and disguises, and the ultimate solution of all entanglements, are adroit pieces of stagecraft, in which features from *Supposes* and *The Taming of a Shrew* are combined with details of the dramatist's own invention. The more narrowly these changes in the underplot are examined, the more ground there is, in my opinion, for assigning their origin to Shakespeare. However this may be, *The Taming of the Shrew*, in spite of Fletcher's counterblast, *The Woman's Prize or the Tamer Tamed*, where Petruchio is reduced to submission by his second wife, Maria, has still a firm place in the affections of readers and playgoers. Its continued popularity in an age which has a very different standard for problems of sex than the Elizabethan, is due not merely to the genius of Shakespeare, but to the genuine dramatic skill and insight of the anonymous writer who gave to the stage *The Taming of a Shrew*.

In concluding this Introduction I must express my sincere thanks to Professor I. Gollancz and Mr. R. B. McKerrow for valuable advice and help; to Dr. F. J. Furnivall for his kindness in placing at my disposal his own copy of Mr. C. Praetorius' facsimile of the quarto of 1594; and to Messrs. Chatto and Windus for permission to reprint, with slight modifications, Appendix III. of this edition from *The Taming of the Shrew* in *The Old-Spelling Shakespeare*.

F. S. B.

A
Pleaſant Conceited
Hiſtorie, called The taming of a Shrew.

As it was ſundry times acted by the *Right honorable the Earle of* Pembrook his ſeruants.

[Short's device with the motto: 'Et usque ad nubes veritas tua.']

Printed at London by Peter Short and *are to be ſold by Cutbert Burbie, at his* ſhop at the Royall Exchange.
1594.

[DRAMATIS PERSONÆ

IN THE INDUCTION

SLY	*A Drunkard*
A Tapster	
A Lord (who calls himself in jest "Simon")	
A Messenger	
TOM, WILL	*Serving-men*
SANDER, TOM, A Boy	*Players*

Serving-men, Huntsmen

IN THE PLAY

JEROBEL	*Duke of Sestos*
AURELIUS	*His Son*
POLIDOR, FERANDO	*Gentlemen of Athens*
ALFONSO	*A rich Citizen of Athens*
PHYLOTUS	*A Merchant of Athens*
VALERIA	*Servant to Aurelius*
A Boy	*Servant to Polidor*
SANDER, TOM, WILL	*Servants to Ferando*
A Tailor	
A Haberdasher	
KATE, PHILEMA, EMELIA	*Daughters to Alfonso*]

A PLEASANT CONCEITED HISTORY

CALLED

THE TAMING OF A SHREW

[INDUCTION

SCENE I.—Before an alehouse in the country.]

Enter a *Tapster*, beating out of his doors *Sly* drunk.

Tapster. *You whoreson drunken slave! you had best be gone,*
And empty your drunken paunch somewhere else,
For in this house thou shalt not rest to-night. [Exit *Tapster*.

Sly. *Tilly vally, by crisee, Tapster, I'll feeze you anon! Fill's the tother pot, and all's paid for! look you, I do drink it of mine own instigation.* Omne bene: *here I'll lie awhile: why, Tapster, I say, fill's a fresh cushion here! Heigh ho, here's good warm lying.* [He falls asleep.

Enter a *Nobleman* and his *men* from hunting.

Lord. *Now that the gloomy shadow of the night,*
Longing to view Orion's drizzling looks,
Leaps from th' Antarctic world unto the sky,
And dims the welkin with her pitchy breath, 12

And darksome night o'ershades the crystal heavens,
Here break we off our hunting for to-night:
Couple up the hounds and let us hie us home,
And bid the huntsmen see them meated well, 16
For they have all deserved it well to-day.
But soft, what sleepy fellow is this lies here?
Or is he dead? See one what he doth lack.

Serving-man. *My lord, 'tis nothing but a drunken sleep; his head is too heavy for his body, and he hath drunk so much that he can go no furder.*

Lord. *Fie, how the slavish villain stinks of drink!*
Ho, sirrah, arise! What, so sound asleep? 24
Go, take him up and bear him to my house,
And bear him easily for fear he wake,
And in my fairest chamber make a fire,
Aud set a sumptuous banquet on the board, 28
And put my richest garments on his back;
Then set him at the table in a chair.
When this is done, against he shall awake,
Let heavenly music play about him still: 32
Go two of you away and bear him hence,
And then I'll tell you what I have devised;
But see in any case you wake him not. [Exeunt *two* with *Sly*.
Now take my cloak and give me one of yours; 36
All fellows now, and see you take me so,
For we will wait upon this drunken man,
To see his count'nance when he doth awake
And find himself clothèd in such attire, 40

With heavenly music sounding in his ears,
And such a banquet set before his eyes,
The fellow sure will think he is in heaven;
But we will be about him when he wakes, 44
And see you call him 'lord' at every word,
And offer thou him his horse to ride abroad,
And thou his hawks and hounds to hunt the deer,
And I will ask what suits he means to wear, 48
And whatsoe'er he saith, see you do not laugh,
But still persuade him that he is a lord.

Enter *one.*

Mes. *And it please your honour, your players be come,*
And do attend your honour's pleasure here. 52
Lord. *The fittest time they could have chosen out;*
Bid one or two of them come hither straight.
Now will I fit myself accordingly,
For they shall play to him when he awakes. 56

Enter *two* of the players with packs at their backs, and a *boy.*

Now, sirs, what store of plays have you?
San. *Marry, my lord, you may have a tragical, or a comodity, or what you will.*
The other. *A comedy, thou should'st say; souns, thou'lt shame us all.*

Lord. *And what's the name of your comedy?*
San. *Marry, my lord, 'tis called 'The Taming of a Shrew'; 'tis a good lesson for us, my lord, for us that are married men.* 64
Lord. *'The Taming of a Shrew,' that's excellent, sure;*
Go see that you make you ready straight,
For you must play before a lord to-night:
Say, you are his men and I your fellow; 68
He's something foolish, bnt whatsoe'er he says,
See that you be not dashed out of countenance.
And, sirrah, go you make you ready straight,
And dress yourself like some lovely lady, 72
And when I call, see that you come to me;
For I will say to him thou art his wife.
Dally with him and hug him in thine arms;
And if he desire to go to bed with thee, 76
Then feign some 'scuse, and say thou wilt anon.
Be gone, I say, and see thou dost it well!
Boy. *Fear not, my lord, I'll dandle him well enough,*
And make him think I love him mightily. [Exit *boy.*
Lord. *Now, sirs, go you and make you ready too,*
For you must play as soon as he doth wake.
San. O *brave, sirrah Tom, we must play before*
A foolish lord, come, let's go make us ready; 84
Go get a dishclout to make clean your shoes,
And I'll speak for the properties. My lord, we must
Have a shoulder of mutton for a property,
And a little vinegar to make our devil roar. 88
Lord. *Very well; sirrah, see that they want nothing.*

[SCENE II.—A room in the lord's house.]

Enter *two* with a table and a banquet on it, and *two others* with *Sly*, asleep in a chair, richly apparelled, and the music playing.

One. *So: sirrah, now go call my lord, and tell him that all things is ready as he willed it.*

Another. *Set thou some wine upon the board, and then I'll go fetch my lord presently.* [Exit.

Enter the *lord* and his *men*.

Lord. *How now! What, is all things ready?*
One. *Ay, my lord.*
Lord. *Then sound the music, and I'll wake him straight;*
And see you do as erst I gave in charge. 8
My lord, my lord! He sleeps soundly. My lord!
Sly. *Tapster, gi's a little small ale. Heigh ho!*
Lord. *Here's wine, my lord, the purest of the grape.*
Sly. *For which lord?* 12
Lord. *For your honour, my lord.*
Sly. *Who, I? Am I a lord?*
Jesus! what fine apparel have I got!
Lord. *More richer far your honour hath to wear,* 16
And if it please you I will fetch them straight.
Wil. *And if your honour please to ride abroad,*
I'll fetch you lusty steeds more swift of pace
Than wingèd Pegasus in all his pride, 20
That ran so swiftly o'er the Persian plains.

Tom. *And if your honour please to hunt the deer,*
Your hounds stand ready coupled at the door;
Who in running will o'ertake the roe, 24
And make the long-breathed tiger broken-winded.

Sly. *By the mass, I think I am a lord indeed.*
What's thy name?

Lord. *Simon, and it please your honour.* 28

Sly. *Simon, that's as much to say 'Simion' or 'Simon,' put forth thy hand and fill the pot.*
Give me thy hand, Sim, am I a lord indeed?

Lord. *Ay, my gracious lord, and your lovely lady* 32
Long time hath mournèd for your absence here,
And now with joy behold where she doth come,
To gratulate your honour's safe return.

Enter the *boy* in woman's attire.

Sly. *Sim, is this she?* 36

Lord. *Ay, my lord.*

Sly. *Mass! 'tis a pretty wench; what's her name?*

Boy. *Oh that my lovely lord would once vouchsafe*
To look on me, and leave these frantic fits; 40
Or were I now but half so eloquent,
To paint in words what I'll perform in deeds,
I know your honour then would pity me.

Sly. *Hark you, mistress, will you eat a piece of bread? Come sit down on my knee. Sim, drink to her, Sim,*
For she and I will go to bed anon.

Lord. *May it please you, your honour's players be come to offer your honour a play.* 48

Sly. *A play, Sim: O brave, be they my players?*

Lord. *Ay, my lord.*

Sly. *Is there not a fool in the play?*

Lord. *Yes, my lord.* 52

Sly. *When will they play, Sim?*

Lord. *Even when it please your honour, they be ready.*

Boy. *My lord, I'll go bid them begin their play.*

Sly. *Do, but look that you come again.* 56

Boy. *I warrant you, my lord, I will not leave you thus.*

[Exit *boy.*

Sly. *Come, Sim, where be the players? Sim, stand by me, and we'll flout the players out of their coats.*

Lord. *I'll call them, my lord. Ho! where are you there?* 60

ACT I

[Scene I.—*Athens: a public place in front of* Alfonso's *house.*]

Sound trumpets.

Enter two young gentlemen, *and a* man *and a* boy.

Pol. Welcome to Athens, my belovèd friend,
To Plato's schools and Aristotle's walks;
Welcome from Sestos, famous for the love
Of good Leander and his tragedy, 4
For whom the Hellespont weeps brinish tears:
The greatest grief is I cannot as I would
Give entertainment to my dearest friend.
Aurel. Thanks, noble Polidor, my second self: 8
The faithful love which I have found in thee
Hath made me leave my father's princely court,
The Duke of Sestos' thrice renownèd seat,
To come to Athens thus to find thee out; 12
Which since I have so happily attained,
My fortune now I do account as great
As erst did Cæsar when he conquered most.
But tell me, noble friend, where shall we lodge, 16
For I am unacquainted in this place.

Poli. My lord, if you vouchsafe of scholar's fare,
My house, my self, and all is yours to use.
You and your men shall stay and lodge with me. 20
Aurel. With all my heart I will requite thy love.

Enter ALFONSO *and his three* daughters.

But stay; what dames are these so bright of hue,
Whose eyes are brighter than the lamps of heaven,
Fairer than rocks of pearl and precious stone, 24
More lovely far than is the morning sun
When first she opes her oriental gates?
Alfon. Daughters, be gone, and hie you to the church,
And I will hie me down unto the quay, 28
To see what merchandise is come ashore.
[*Exeunt* ALFONSO *and his three* daughters.
Pol. Why, how now, my lord? What, in a dump
To see these damsels pass away so soon?
Aurel. Trust me, my friend, I must confess to thee, 32
I took so much delight in these fair dames,
As I do wish they had not gone so soon;
But, if thou canst, resolve me what they be,
And what old man it was that went with them, 36
For I do long to see them once again.
Pol. I cannot blame your honour, good my lord,
For they are both lovely, wise, fair and young,
And one of them, the youngest of the three, 40
I long have lov'd (sweet friend) and she lov'd me;

But never yet we could not find a means
How we might compass our desirèd joys.
Aurel. Why, is not her father willing to the match? 44
Pol. Yes, trust me, but he hath solemnly sworn
His eldest daughter first shall be espoused,
Before he grants his youngest leave to love;
And, therefore, he that means to get their loves 48
Must first provide for her if he will speed;
And he that hath her shall be fretted so
As good be wedded to the devil himself,
For such a scold as she did never live; 52
And till that she be sped none else can speed,
Which makes me think that all my labour's lost:
And whosoe'er can get her firm good will,
A large dowry he shall be sure to have, 56
For her father is a man of mighty wealth,
And an ancient citizen of the town,
And that was he that went along with them.
Aurel. But he shall keep her still by my advice; 60
And yet I needs must love his second daughter,
The image of honour and nobility,
In whose sweet person is comprised the sum
Of nature's skill and heavenly majesty. 64
Pol. I like your choice, and glad you chose not mine.
Then if you like to follow on your love,
We must devise a means and find some one
That will attempt to wed this devilish scold, 68
And I do know the man. Come hither, boy;

Go your ways, sirrah, to Ferando's house,
Desire him take the pains to come to me,
For I must speak with him immediately. 72

Boy. I will, sir, and fetch him presently.

Pol. A man, I think, will fit her humour right,
As blunt in speech as she is sharp of tongue,
And he, I think, will match her every way: 76
And yet he is a man of wealth sufficient,
And for his person worth as good as she;
And if he compassed her to be his wife,
Then may we freely visit both our loves. 80

Aurel. Oh, might I see the centre of my soul,
Whose sacred beauty hath enchanted me,
More fair than was the Grecian Helena
For whose sweet sake so many princes died, 84
That came with thousand ships to Tenedos!
But when we come unto her father's house,
Tell him I am a merchant's son of Sestos,
That comes for traffic unto Athens here, 88
And here, sirrah, I will change with you for once.
And now be thou the Duke of Sestos' son;
Revel and spend as if thou wert myself,
For I will court my love in this disguise. 92

Val. My lord, how if the duke, your father, should
By some means come to Athens for to see
How you do profit in these public schools,
And find me clothèd thus in your attire, 96
How would he take it then, think you, my lord?

Aurel. Tush, fear not, Valeria, let me alone;
But stay, here comes some other company.

Enter FERANDO, *and his man* SANDER *with a blue coat.*

Pol. Here comes the man that I did tell you of. 100
Feran. Good morrow, gentlemen, to all at once!
How now, Polidor; what, man, still in love?
Ever wooing and canst thou never speed?
God send me better luck when I shall woo. 104
San. I warrant you, master, and you take my counsel.
Feran. Why, sirrah, are you so cunning?
San. Who, I? 'Twere better for you by five mark, and you could tell how to do it as well as I. 108
Pol. I would thy master once were in the vein
To try himself how he could woo a wench.
Feran. Faith, I am even now a-going.
San. I'faith, sir, my master's going to this gear now. 112
Pol. Whither, in faith, Ferando? Tell me true.
Feran. To bonny Kate, the patientest wench alive—
The devil himself dares scarce venture to woo her—
Signor Alfonso's eldest daughter: 116
And he hath promised me six thousand crowns
If I can win her once to be my wife.
And she and I must woo with scolding sure,
And I will hold her to't till she be weary, 120
Or else I'll make her yield to grant me love.
Pol. How like you this, Aurelius? I think he knew

Our minds before we sent to him.
But tell me, when do you mean to speak with her? 124
Feran. Faith, presently. Do you but stand aside,
And I will make her father bring her hither,
And she, and I, and he, will talk alone.
Pol. With all our hearts! Come, Aurelius, 128
Let us be gone, and leave him here alone. [*Exit.*
Feran. Ho! Signor Alfonso, who's within there?
Alfon. Signor Ferando, you're welcome heartily;
You are a stranger, sir, unto my house. 132
Hark you, sir, look, what I did promise you
I'll perform, if you get my daughter's love.
Feran. Then when I have talked a word or two with her,
Do you step in and give her hand to me, 136
And tell her when the marriage day shall be;
For I do know she would be married fain:
And when our nuptial rites be once performed,
Let me alone to tame her well enough. 140
Now call her forth that I may speak with her.

Enter KATE.

Alfon. Ha, Kate! Come hither, wench, and list to me.
Use this gentleman friendly as thou canst.
Feran. Twenty good morrows to my lovely Kate! 144
Kate. You jest, I am sure; is she yours already?
Feran. I tell thee, Kate, I know thou lov'st me well.

Kate. The devil you do! Who told you so?
Feran. My mind, sweet Kate, doth say I am the man 148
Must wed, and bed, and marry bonny Kate.
Kate. Was ever seen so gross an ass as this?
Feran. Ay, to stand so long and never get a kiss.
Kate. Hands off, I say, and get you from this place; 152
Or I will set my ten commandments in your face.
Feran. I prithee do, Kate; they say thou art a shrew,
And I like thee the better, for I would have thee so.
Kate. Let go my hand for fear it reach your ear. 156
Feran. No, Kate, this hand is mine, and I thy love.
Kate. In faith, sir, no; the woodcock wants his tail.
Feran. But yet his bill will serve, if the other fail.
Alfon. How now, Ferando, what says my daughter? 160
Feran. She's willing, sir, and loves me as her life.
Kate. 'Tis for your skin then, but not to be your wife.
Alfon. Come hither, Kate, and let me give thy hand
To him that I have chosen for thy love, 164
And thou to-morrow shalt be wed to him.
Kate. Why, father, what do you mean to do with me,
To give me thus unto this brain-sick man,
That in his mood cares not to murder me? 168
[*She turns aside and speaks.*
But yet I will consent and marry him,
For I methinks have lived too long a maid,
And match him too, or else his manhood's good.
Alfon. Give me thy hand. Ferando loves thee well, 172
And will with wealth and ease maintain thy state.

Here, Ferando, take her for thy wife,
And Sunday next shall be your wedding day.
Feran. Why so, did I not tell thee I should be the man?
Father, I leave my lovely Kate with you:
Provide yourselves against our marriage day;
For I must hie me to my country house
In haste, to see provision may be made 180
To entertain my Kate when she doth come.
Alfon. Do so. Come, Kate, why dost thou look so sad?
Be merry, wench, thy wedding day's at hand,
Son, fare you well, and see you keep your promise. 184
[*Exeunt* ALFONSO *and* KATE.
Feran. So: all, thus far, goes well. Ho, Sander!

Enter SANDER, *laughing.*

San. Sander, i'faith you're a beast, I cry God heartily mercy; my heart's ready to run out of my belly with laughing. I stood behind the door all this while and heard what you said to her.
Feran. Why, did'st thou think that I did not speak well to her?
San. You spoke like an ass to her; I'll tell you what, and I had been there to have wooed her, and had this cloak on that you have, chud have had her before she had gone a step furder; and you talk of woodcocks with her, and I I cannot tell you what. 196

Feran. Well, sirrah, and yet thou seest I have got her for all this.

San. Ay, marry, 'twas more by hap than any good cunning: I hope she'll make you one of the head men of the parish shortly.

Feran. Well, sirrah, leave your jesting and go to Polidor's house,
The young gentleman that was here with me,
And tell him the circumstance of all thou know'st, 204
Tell him on Sunday next we must be married;
And if he ask thee whither I am gone,
Tell him into the country, to my house,
And upon Sunday I'll be here again. 208

[*Exit* FERANDO.

San. I warrant you, master, fear not me for doing of my business. Now hang him that has not a livery coat to slash it out and swash it out amongst the proudest on them. Why look you now, I'll scarce put up plain 'Sander' now at any of their hands, for and anybody have anything to do with my master, straight they come crouching upon me, 'I beseech you, good Master Sander, speak a good word for me,' and then am I so stout and takes it upon me, and stands upon my pantoffles to them out of all cry; why, I have a life like a giant now, but that my master hath such a pestilent mind to a woman now a late, and I have a pretty wench to my sister, and I had thought to have preferred my master to her, and that would have been a good deal in my way, but that he's sped already.

Enter POLIDOR's boy.

Boy. Friend, well met!

San. Souns, 'Friend, well met!' I hold my life he sees not my master's livery coat. Plain friend hop-of-my-thumb, know you who we are?

Boy. Trust me, sir, it is the use where I was born to salute men after this manner; yet, notwithstanding, if you be angry with me for calling of you 'friend,' I am the more sorry for it, hoping the style of a fool will make you amends for all.

San. The slave is sorry for his fault, now we cannot be angry. Well, what's the matter that you would do with us.

Boy. Marry, sir, I hear you pertain to Signor Ferando.

San. Ay, and thou beest not blind, thou mayest see; *Ecce signum*, here.

Boy. Shall I entreat you to do me a message to your master?

San. Ay, it may be, and you tell us from whence you come.

Boy. Marry, sir, I serve young Polidor, your master's friend.

San. Do you serve him, and what's your name? 244

Boy. My name, sirrah, I tell thee, sirrah, is called Catapie.

San. Cake and pie? Oh, my teeth waters to have a piece of thee. 248

Boy. Why, slave, would'st thou eat me?

San. Eat thee, who would not eat cake and pie?

Boy. Why, villain, my name is Catapie. But wilt thou tell me where thy master is? 252

San. Nay, thou must first tell me where thy master is, for I have good news for him, I can tell thee.

Boy. Why, see where he comes.

Enter POLIDOR, AURELIUS, *and* VALERIA.

Pol. Come, sweet Aurelius, my faithful friend, 256
Now will we go to see those lovely dames,
Richer in beauty than the orient pearl,
Whiter than is the Alpine crystal mould,
And far more lovely than the Terean plant, 260
That blushing in the air turns to a stone.
What, Sander, what news with you?

San. Marry, sir, my master sends you word that you must come to his wedding to-morrow. 264

Pol. What, shall he be married then?

San. Faith, ay: you think he stands as long about it as you do?

Pol. Whither is thy master gone now? 268

San. Marry, he's gone to our house in the country, to make all things in a readiness against my new mistress comes thither, but he'll come again to-morrow.

Pol. This is suddenly despatched belike. 272
Well, sirrah, boy, take Sander in with you,
And have him to the buttery presently.

Boy. I will, sir: come, Sander.

[*Exeunt* SANDER *and the* boy.

Aurel. Valeria, as erst we did devise, 276
Take thou thy lute and go to Alfonso's house,
And say that Polidor sent thee thither.

Pol. Ay, Valeria, for he spoke to me,
To help him to some cunning musician 280
To teach his eldest daughter on the lute;
And thou, I know, wilt fit his turn so well,
As thou shalt get great favour at his hands:
Begone, Valeria, and say I sent thee to him. 284

Vale. I will, sir, and stay your coming at Alfonso's house.

[*Exit* VALERIA.

Pol. Now, sweet Aurelius, by this device
Shall we have leisure for to court our loves;
For whilst that she is learning on the lute, 288
Her sisters may take time to steal abroad;
For otherwise she'll keep them both within,
And make them work whilst she herself doth play.
But come, let's go unto Alfonso's house, 292
And see how Valeria and Kate agrees;
I doubt his music scarce will please his scholar.
But stay, here comes Alfonso.

Enter ALFONSO.

Alfon. What, Master Polidor, you are well met; 296
I thank you for the man you sent to me,

A good musician, I think he is,
I have set my daughter and him together.
But is this gentleman a friend of yours? 300
Pol. He is; I pray you, sir, bid him welcome.
He's a wealthy merchant's son of Sestos.
Alfon. You're welcome, sir, and if my house afford
You anything that may content your mind, 304
I pray you, sir, make bold with me.
Aurel. I thank you, sir, and if what I have got,
By merchandise or travel on the seas,
Satins, or lawns, or azure-coloured silk, 308
Or precious fiery pointed stones of Indie,
You shall command both them, myself, and all.
Alfon. Thanks, gentle sir; Polidor, take him in,
And bid him welcome, too, unto my house, 312
For thou, I think, must be my second son.
Ferando—Polidor, dost thou not know?—
Must marry Kate; and to-morrow is the day.
Pol. Such news I heard, and I came now to know. 316
Alfon. Polidor, 'tis true, go, let me alone,
For I must see against the bridegroom come,
That all things be according to his mind,
And so I'll leave you for an hour or two. 320
[*Exit.*

Pol. Come then, Aurelius, come in with me,
And we'll go sit awhile and chat with them,
And after bring them forth to take the air.

[*Exit.*

Then *Sly* speaks.

Sly. *Sim, when will the fool come again?* 324

Lord. *He'll come again, my Lord, anon.*

Sly. *Gi's some more drink here; souns, where's the Tapster? Here, Sim, eat some of these things.*

Lord. *So I do, my Lord.* 328

Sly. *Here, Sim, I drink to thee.*

Lord. *My Lord, here comes the players again.*

Sly. *O brave, here's two fine gentlewomen!*

ACT II

[SCENE I.—*A room in* Alfonso's *house.*]

Enter VALERIA *with a lute, and* KATE *with him.*

Val. The senseless trees by music have been moved,
And at the sound of pleasant tunèd strings,
Have savage beasts hung down their list'ning heads,
As though they had been cast into a trance: 4
Then it may be that she whom nought can please,
With music's sound in time may be surprised.
Come, lovely mistress, will you take your lute,
And play the lesson that I taught you last? 8

Kate. It is no matter whether I do or no,
For, trust me, I take no great delight in it.

Val. I would, sweet mistress, that it lay in me
To help you to that thing that's your delight. 12

Kate. In you, with a pestilence, are you so kind?
Then make a night-cap of your fiddle's case,
To warm your head, and hide your filthy face.

Val. If that, sweet mistress, were your heart's content, 16
You should command a greater thing than that,
Although it were ten times to my disgrace.

Kate. You're so kind, 'twere pity you should be hang'd;
And yet methinks the fool doth look asquint. 20
Val. Why, mistress, do you mock me?
Kate. No, but I mean to move thee.
Val. Well, will you play a little?
Kate. Ay, give me the lute. 24
[*She plays.*
Val. That stop was false, play it again.
Kate. Then mend it thou, thou filthy ass!
Val. What, do you bid me kiss your arse?
Kate. How now, Jack Sauce, you're a jolly mate; 28
You're best be still, lest I cross your pate,
And make your music fly about your ears;
I'll make it and your foolish coxcomb meet.
[*She offers to strike him with the lute.*
Val. Hold, mistress; souns, will you break my lute? 32
Kate. Ay, on thy head, and if thou speak to me:
There, take it up, and fiddle somewhere else.
[*She throws it down.*
And see you come no more into this place,
Lest that I clap your fiddle on your face. 36
[*Exit* KATE.
Val. Souns, teach her to play upon the lute?
The devil shall teach her first; I am glad she's gone,
For I was ne'er so 'fraid in all my life,
But that my lute should fly about mine ears. 40
My master shall teach her his self for me,
For I'll keep me far enough without her reach:

For he and Polidor sent me before,
To be with her and teach her on the lute, 44
Whilst they did court the other gentlewomen,
And here methinks they come together.

Enter AURELIUS, POLIDOR, EMELIA, *and* PHILEMA.

Pol. How now, Valeria, where's your mistress?
Val. At the vengeance, I think, and nowhere else. 48
Aurel. Why, Valeria, will she not learn apace?
Val. Yes, by'r lady, she has learnt too much already;
And that I had felt, had I not spoke her fair:
But she shall ne'er be learnt for me again. 52
Aurel. Well, Valeria, go to my chamber,
And bear him company that came to-day
From Sestos, where our aged father dwells. [*Exit* VALERIA.
Pol. Come, fair Emelia, my lovely love, 56
Brighter than the burnished palace of the sun,
The eyesight of the glorious firmament,
In whose bright looks sparkles the radiant fire,
Wily Prometheus slily stole from Jove, 60
Infusing breath, life, motion, soul,
To every object stricken by thine eyes!
O fair Emelia, I pine for thee,
And either must enjoy thy love, or die. 64
Eme. Fie, man, I know you will not die for love.
Ah, Polidor, thou needst not to complain;
Eternal heaven sooner be dissolved,

And all that pierceth Phœbus' silver eye, 68
Before such hap befall to Polidor.
Pol. Thanks, fair Emelia, for these sweet words;
But what saith Philema to her friend?
Phile. Why, I am buying merchandise of him. 72
Aurel. Mistress, you shall not need to buy of me,
For when I crossed the bubbling Canibey,
And sailed along the crystal Hellespont,
I filled my coffers of the wealthy mines, 76
Where I did cause millions of labouring Moors
To undermine the caverns of the earth,
To seek for strange and new-found precious stones,
And dive into the sea to gather pearl, 80
As fair as Juno offered Priam's son;
And you shall take your liberal choice of all.
Phile. I thank you, sir, and would Philema might
In any curtesy requite you so, 84
As she with willing heart could well bestow!

Enter ALFONSO.

Alfon. How now, daughters, is Ferando come?
Eme. Not yet, father. I wonder he stays so long.
Alfon. And where's your sister, that she is not here? 88
Phile. She is making of her ready, father,
To go to church, and if that he were come.
Pol. I warrant you, he'll not be long away.
Alfon. Go, daughters, get you in, and bid your sister 92

Provide herself against that we do come,
And see you go to church along with us.
[*Exeunt* PHILEMA *and* EMELIA.
I marvel that Ferando comes not away.
Pol. His tailor, it may be, hath been too slack 96
In his apparel which he means to wear;
For no question but some fantastic suits
He is determinèd to wear to-day,
And richly powderèd with precious stones, 100
Spotted with liquid gold, thick set with pearl,
And such he means shall be his wedding suits.
Alfon. I cared not, I, what cost he did bestow,
In gold or silk, so he himself were here, 104
For I had rather lose a thousand crowns,
Than that he should deceive us here to-day:
But soft, I think I see him come.

Enter FERANDO, *basely attired, and a red cap on his head.*

Feran. Good morrow, father; Polidor, well met; 108
You wonder, I know, that I have stayed so long.
Alfon. Ay, marry, son, we were almost persuaded,
That we should scarce have had our bridegroom here.
But say, why art thou thus basely attired? 112
Feran. Thus richly, father, you should have said;
For when my wife and I am married once,
She's such a shrew, if we should once fall out
She'll pull my costly suits over mine ears, 116

And therefore am I thus attired awhile;
For many things I tell you's in my head,
And none must know thereof but Kate and I;
For we shall live like lambs and lions, sure; 120
Nor lambs to lions never was so tame,
If once they lie within the lion's paws,
As Kate to me if we were married once,
And therefore come, let us to church presently. 124
Pol. Fie, Ferando; not thus attired, for shame!
Come to my chamber and there suit thyself
Of twenty suits that I did never wear.
Feran. Tush, Polidor, I have as many suits 128
Fantastic made to fit my humour so
As any in Athens and as richly wrought
As was the massy robe that late adorned
The stately legate of the Persian King; 132
And this from them have I made choice to wear.
Alfon. I prithee, Ferando, let me entreat,
Before thou go'st unto the church with us,
To put some other suit upon thy back. 136
Feran. Not for the world, if I might gain it so:
And therefore take me thus, or not at all.

Enter KATE.

But soft, see where my Kate doth come!
I must salute her: how fares my lovely Kate? 140
What, art thou ready? shall we go to church?

Kate. Not I, with one so mad, so basely 'tired,
To marry such a filthy, slavish groom,
That, as it seems, sometimes is from his wits, 144
Or else he would not thus have come to us.

Feran. Tush, Kate, these words adds greater love in me,
And makes me think thee fairer than before:
Sweet Kate, lovelier than Diana's purple robe, 148
Whiter than are the snowy Apennines,
Or icy hair that grows on Boreas' chin!
Father, I swear by Ibis' golden beak,
More fair and radiant is my bonny Kate, 152
Than silver Xanthus, when he doth embrace
The ruddy Simois at Ida's feet.
And care not thou, sweet Kate, how I be clad;
Thou shalt have garments wrought of Median silk, 156
Enchased with precious jewels fetched from far,
By Italian merchants that with Russian stems
Ploughs up huge furrows in the Terrene Maine,
And better far my lovely Kate shall wear. 160
Then come, sweet love, and let us to the church,
For this I swear shall be my wedding suit.

[*Exit* KATE.

Alfon. Come, gentlemen, go along with us;
For thus, do what we can, he will be wed. 164

[*Exeunt Omnes.*

[SCENE II.—*A room in* Alfonso's *house*.]

Enter POLIDOR'S boy *and* SANDER.

Boy. Come hither, sirrah boy.

San. Boy, oh, disgrace to my person! Souns! boy, of your face! You have many boys with such pickadevants, I am sure! Souns, would you not have a bloody nose for this?

Boy. Come, come, I did but jest; where is that same piece of pie that I gave thee to keep?

San. The pie? Ay, you have more mind of your belly than to go see what your master does. 8

Boy. Tush, 'tis no matter, man, I prithee give it me; I am very hungry, I promise thee.

San. Why, you may take it, and the devil burst you with it! One cannot save a bit after supper but you are always ready to munch it up.

Boy. Why come, man, we shall have good cheer anon at the bridehouse, for your master's gone to church to be married already, and there's such cheer as passeth. 16

San. O brave, I would I had eat no meat this week, for I have never a corner left in my belly to put a venison pasty in; I think I shall burst myself with eating, for I'll so cram me down the tarts and the marchpanes, out of all cry. 20

Boy. Ay, but how wilt thou do, now thy master's married? Thy mistress is such a devil as she'll make thee forget thy eating quickly; she'll beat thee so.

San. Let my master alone with her for that, for he'll make her tame well enough ere long, I warrant thee; for he's such a churl waxen now of late, that, and he be never so little angry, he thums me out of all cry. But in my mind, sirrah, the youngest is a very pretty wench, and if I thought thy master would not have her, I'd have a fling at her myself. I'll see soon whether 'twill be a match or no; and it will not, I'll set the matter hard for myself, I warrant thee. 31

Boy. Souns, you slave, will you be a rival with my master in his love? Speak but such another word and I'll cut off one of thy legs.

San. Oh, cruel judgment! nay then, sirrah, my tongue shall talk no more to you: marry, my timber shall tell the trusty message of his master even on the very forehead of thee, thou abusious villain: therefore prepare thyself. 38

Boy. Come hither, thou imperfectious slave in regard of thy beggary; hold thee, there's two shillings for thee, to pay for the healing of thy left leg, which I mean furiously to invade, or to maim at the least.

San. Oh, supernodical fool! Well, I'll take your two shillings; but I'll bar striking at legs. 44

Boy. Not I, for I'll strike anywhere.

San. Here, here, take your two shillings again. I'll see thee hanged ere I'll fight with thee; I gat a broken shin the other day, 'tis not whole yet, and therefore I'll not fight; come, come, why should we fall out? 49

Boy. Well, sirrah, your fair words hath something allayed my choler: I am content for this once to put it up and be friends with thee. But soft, see where they come all from church, belike they be married already. 53

Enter Ferando, Kate, Alfonso, Polidor, Emelia, Aurelius, *and* Philema.

Feran. Father, farewell! my Kate and I must home.
Sirrah, go make ready my horse presently.

Alfon. Your horse? What, son, I hope you do but jest!
I am sure you will not go so suddenly. 57

Kate. Let him go or tarry, I am resolved to stay,
And not to travel on my wedding-day.

Feran. Tut, Kate, I tell thee we must needs go home.
Villain, hast thou saddled my horse?

San. Which horse? your curtal?

Feran. Souns, you slave, stand you prating here? Saddle the bay gelding for your mistress. 64

Kate. Not for me: for I'll not go.

San. The ostler will not let me have him. You owe tenpence for his meat, and sixpence for stuffing my mistress' saddle. 68

Feran. Here, villain, go pay him straight.

San. Shall I give them another peck of lavender?

Feran. Out, slave, and bring them presently to the door! 72

Alfon. Why, son, I hope at least you'll dine with us!

San. I pray you, master, let's stay till dinner be done.

Feran. Souns, villain, art thou here yet?

[*Exit* Sander.

Come, Kate, our dinner is provided at home. 76

Kate. But not for me; for here I mean to dine.

I'll have my will in this as well as you:
Though you in madding mood would leave your friends,
Despite of you, I'll tarry with them still. 80

Feran. Ay, Kate, so thou shalt, but at some other time.
Whenas thy sisters here shall be espoused,
Then thou and I will keep our wedding-day
In better sort than now we can provide; 84
For here I promise thee before them all,
We will ere long return to them again.
Come, Kate, stand not on terms, we will away;
This is my day; to-morrow thou shalt rule, 88
And I will do whatever thou commands.
Gentlemen, farewell; we'll take our leaves:
It will be late before that we come home.

[*Exeunt* FERANDO *and* KATE.

Pol. Farewell, Ferando, since you will be gone! 92

Alfon. So mad a couple did I never see.

Eme. They're even as well matched as I would wish.

Phile. And yet I hardly think that he can tame her;
For when he has done she will do what she list. 96

Aurel. Her manhood then is good, I do believe.

Pol. Aurelius, or else I miss my mark,
Her tongue will walk if she doth hold her hands.
I am in doubt ere half a month be passed 100
He'll curse the priest that married him so soon.
And yet it may be she will be reclaimed,
For she is very patient grown of late.

Alfon. God hold it that it may continue still! 104
I would be loath that they should disagree;
But he, I hope, will hold her in a while.
Pol. Within this two days I will ride to him,
And see how lovingly they do agree. 108
Alfon. Now, Aurelius, what say you to this?
What, have you sent to Sestos, as you said,
To certify your father of your love?
For I would gladly he would like of it; 112
And if he be the man you tell to me,
I guess he is a merchant of great wealth;
And I have seen him oft at Athens here,
And for his sake assure thee thou art welcome. 116
Pol. And so to me, whilst Polidor doth live.
Aurel. I find it so, right worthy gentlemen,
And of what worth your friendship I esteem,
I leave censure of your several thoughts. 120
But for requital of your favours past,
Rests yet behind, which, when occasion serves,
I vow shall be remembered to the full;
And for my father's coming to this place, 124
I do expect within this week at most.
Alfon. Enough, Aurelius! but we forget
Our marriage dinner now the bride is gone;
Come let us see what there they left behind. 128
[*Exeunt Omnes.*

ACT III

[SCENE I.—*A room in* Ferando's *country house.*]

Enter SANDER *with two or three* Serving men.

San. Come, sirs, provide all things as fast as you can, for my master's hard at hand and my new mistress and all, and he sent me before to see all things ready.

Tom. Welcome home, Sander! Sirrah, how looks our new mistress? they say she's a plaguey shrew.

San. Ay, and that thou shalt find, I can tell thee, and thou dost not please her well; why, my master has such ado with her as it passeth, and he's even like a madman. 8

Will. Why, Sander, what does he say?

San. Why, I'll tell you what: when they should go to church to be married he puts on an old jerkin and a pair of canvas breeches down to the small of his leg and a red cap on his head, and he looks as thou wilt burst thyself with laughing when thou seest him: he's e'en as good as a fool for me: and then, when they should go to dinner, he made me saddle the horse, and away he came, and ne'er tarried for dinner: and therefore you had best get supper ready against they come, for they be hard at hand, I am sure, by this time.

Tom. Souns, see where they be all ready. 20

Enter FERANDO *and* KATE.

Feran. Now welcome, Kate! where's these villains?
Here, what, not supper yet upon the board;
Nor table spread, nor nothing done at all?
Where's that villain that I sent before? 24

San. Now, *adsum*, sir.

Feran. Come hither, you villain, I'll cut your nose, you rogue! help me off with my boots: will't please you to lay the cloth? Souns, the villain hurts my foot! Pull easily, I say; yet again!

[*He beats them all. They cover the board and fetch in the meat.*

Souns! Burnt and scorched! Who dressed this meat?

Will. Forsooth, John cook.

[*He throws down the table and meat and all, and beats them.*

Feran. Go, you villains, bring you me such meat? 32
Out of my sight, I say, and bear it hence!
Come, Kate, we'll have other meat provided.
Is there a fire in my chamber, sir?

San. Ay, forsooth. 36

[*Exeunt* FERANDO *and* KATE.

Manent Serving-men *and eat up all the meat.*

Tom. Souns! I think, of my conscience, my master's mad since he was married.

Will. I laughed what a box he gave Sander for pulling off his boots. 40

Enter FERANDO *again.*

San. I hurt his foot for the nonce, man.

Feran. Did you so, you damned villain?

[*He beats them all out again.*

This humour must I hold me to awhile,
To bridle and hold back my headstrong wife, 44
With curbs of hunger, ease, and want of sleep.
Nor sleep nor meat shall she enjoy to-night,
I'll mew her up as men do mew their hawks,
And make her gently come unto the lure. 48
Were she as stubborn or as full of strength
As were the Thracian horse Alcides tamed,
That King Egeus fed with flesh of men,
Yet would I pull her down and make her come 52
As hungry hawks do fly unto their lure. [*Exit.*

[SCENE II.—*Athens: a street.*]

Enter AURELIUS *and* VALERIA.

Aurel. Valeria, attend: I have a lovely love,
As bright as is the heaven crystalline,
As fair as is the milkwhite way of Jove,
As chaste as Phœbe in her summer sports, 4

As soft and tender as the azure down,
That circles Cytherea's silver doves.
Her do I mean to make my lovely bride,
And in her bed to breathe the sweet content, 8
That I, thou know'st, long time have aimèd at.
Now, Valeria, it rests in thee to help
To compass this, that I might gain my love,
Which easily thou may'st perform at will, 12
If that the merchant which thou told'st me of,
Will, as he said, go to Alfonso's house,
And say he is my father, and therewithal
Pass over certain deeds of land to me, 16
That I thereby may gain my heart's desire;
And he is promisèd reward of me.
Val. Fear not, my lord, I'll fetch him straight to you,
For he'll do anything that you command: 20
But tell me, my lord, is Ferando married then?
Aurel. He is: and Polidor shortly shall be wed,
And he means to tame his wife ere long.
Val. He says so. 24
Aurel. Faith, he's gone unto the taming school.
Val. The taming school; why, is there such a place?
Aurel. Ay, and Ferando is the master of the school.
Val. That's rare: but what decorum does he use? 28
Aurel. Faith, I know not, but by some odd device
Or other. But come, Valeria, I long to see the man,
By whom we must comprise our plotted drift,
That I may tell him what we have to do. 32

Val. Then come, my lord, and I will bring you to him straight.

Aurel. Agreed, then let's go. [*Exeunt.*

[SCENE III.—*A room in* Ferando's *country honse.*]

Enter SANDER *and his mistress.*

San. Come, mistress.

Kate. Sander, I prithee, help me to some meat,
I am so faint that I can scarcely stand.

San. Ay, marry, mistress, but you know my master has given me a charge that you must eat nothing but that which he himself giveth you.

Kate. Why, man, thy master needs never know it!

San. You say true, indeed: why, look you, mistress, what say you to a piece of beef and mustard now?

Kate. Why, I say 'tis excellent meat; can'st thou help me to some?

San. I could help you to some, but that I doubt the mustard is too choleric for you. But what say you to a sheep's head and garlic?

Kate. Why, anything; I care not what it be.

San. Ay, but the garlic, I doubt, will make your breath stink, and then my master will course me for letting you eat it. But what say you to a fat capon?

Kate. That's meat for a king; sweet Sander, help me to some of it. 20

San. Nay, by'r lady, then 'tis too dear for us; we must not meddle with the king's meat.

Kate. Out, villain, dost thou mock me? Take that for thy sauciness. [*She beats him.*

San. Souns, are you so light-fingered, with a murrain? I'll keep you fasting for it this two days!

Kate. I tell thee, villain, I'll tear the flesh off thy face and eat it, and thou prates to me thus. 28

San. Here comes my master: now he'll course you.

Enter FERANDO *with a piece of meat upon his dagger's point, and* POLIDOR *with him.*

Feran. See here, Kate, I have provided meat for thee;
Here, take it; what, is't not worthy thanks?
Go, sirrah, take it away again. 32
You shall be thankful for the next you have.

Kate. Why, I thank you for it.

Feran. Nay, now 'tis not worth a pin. Go, sirrah, and take it hence, I say. 36

San. Yes, sir, I'll carry it hence. Master, let her have none, for she can fight, as hungry as she is.

Pol. I pray you, sir, let it stand, for I'll eat some with her myself. 40

Feran. Well, sirrah, set it down again.

Kate. Nay, nay, I pray you let him take it hence,
And keep it for your own diet, for I'll none;
I'll ne'er be beholding to you for your meat; 44

I tell thee flatly here unto thy teeth,
Thou shalt not keep me nor feed me as thou list,
For I will home again unto my father's house.
Feran. Ay, when you're meek and gentle, but not before;
I know your stomach is not yet come down;
Therefore no marvel thou can'st not eat,
And I will go unto your father's house;
Come, Polidor, let us go in again; 52
And, Kate, come in with us! I know ere long
That thou and I shall lovingly agree. [*Exeunt Omnes.*

[Scene IV.—*Athens: a public place in front of* Alfonso's *house.*]

Enter Aurelius, Valeria *and* Phylotus, *the merchant.*

Aurel. Now, Signor Phylotus, we will go
Unto Alfonso's house, and be sure you say
As I did tell you concerning the man
That dwells in Sestos, whose son I said I was, 4
For you do very much resemble him:
And fear not; you may be bold to speak your mind.
Phylo. I warrant you, sir, take you no care;
I'll use myself so cunning in the cause, 8
As you shall soon enjoy your heart's delight.
Aurel. Thanks, sweet Phylotus, then stay you here,
And I will go and fetch him hither straight.
Ho, Signor Alfonso, a word with you. 12

Enter Alfonso.

Alfon. Who's there? What, Aurelius, what's the matter,
That you stand so like a stranger at the door?
Aurel. My father, sir, is newly come to town,
And I have brought him here to speak with you, 16
Concerning those matters that I told you of,
And he can certify you of the truth.
Alfon. Is this your father? You are welcome, sir.
Phylo. Thanks, Alfonso, for that's your name, I guess. 20
I understand my son hath set his mind
And bent his liking to your daughter's love;
And for because he is my only son,
And I would gladly that he should do well, 24
I tell you, sir, I not mislike his choice.
If you agree to give him your consent,
He shall have living to maintain his state;
Three hundred pounds a year I will assure 28
To him and to his heirs: and if they do join,
And knit themselves in holy wedlock band,
A thousand massy ingots of pure gold,
And twice as many bars of silver plate, 32
I freely give him, and in writing straight
I will confirm what I have said in words.
Alfon. Trust me, I must commend your liberal mind,
And loving care you bear unto your son; 36
And here I give him freely my consent.
As for my daughter, I think he knows her mind:

And I will enlarge her dowry for your sake;
And solemnise with joy your nuptial rites. 40
But is this gentleman of Sestos, too?

Aurel. He is the Duke of Sestos' thrice renownèd son,
Who for the love his honour bears to me
Hath thus accompanied me to this place. 44

Alfon. You were to blame you told me not before:
Pardon me, my lord, for if I had known
Your honour had been here in place with me,
I would have done my duty to your honour. 48

Val. Thanks, good Alfonso: but I did come to see
Whenas these marriage rites should be performed;
And if in these nuptials you vouchsafe
To honour thus the prince of Sestos' friend, 52
In celebration of his spousal rites,
He shall remain a lasting friend to you.
What says Aurelius' father?

Phylo. I humbly thank your honour, good my lord; 56
And ere we part, before your honour here,
Shall articles of such content be drawn,
As 'twixt our houses and posterities,
Eternally this league of peace shall last, 60
Inviolate and pure on either part.

Alfon. With all my heart, and if your honour please,
To walk along with us unto my house,
We will confirm these leagues of lasting love. 64

Val. Come then, Aurelius, I will go with you.

[*Exeunt Omnes.*

[SCENE V.—*A room in* Ferando's *country house.*]

Enter FERANDO, KATE, *and* SANDER.

San. Master, the haberdasher has brought my mistress home her cap here.

Enter the Haberdasher.

Feran. Come hither, sirrah! What have you there?
Haber. A velvet cap, sir, and it please you. 4
Feran. Who spoke for it? Didst thou, Kate?
Kate. What if I did? Come hither, sirrah, give me the cap! I'll see if it will fit me. [*She sets it on her head.*
Feran. O monstrous, why, it becomes thee not; 8
Let me see it, Kate! Here, sirrah, take it hence!
This cap is out of fashion quite!
Kate. The fashion is good enough. Belike you mean
To make a fool of me. 12
Feran. Why, true, he means to make a fool of thee,
To have thee put on such a curtailed cap!
Sirrah, begone with it! [*Exit* Haberdasher.

Enter the Tailor *with a gown.*

San. Here is the Tailor too with my mistress' gown. 16
Feran. Let me see it, tailor! What, with cuts and jags,
Souns, you villain, thou hast spoilt the gown!

Tailor. Why, sir, I made it as your man gave me direction. You may read the note here.

Feran. Come hither, sirrah tailor! Read the note.

Tailor. Item, a fair round-compassed cape.

San. Ay, that's true. 24

Tailor. And a large trunk sleeve.

San. That's a lie, master! I said two trunk sleeves.

Feran. Well, sir, go forward!

Tailor. Item, a loose-bodied gown. 28

San. Master, if ever I said loose body's gown, sew me in a seam and beat me to death with [a] bottom of brown thread!

Tailor. I made it as the note bade me. 32

San. I say the note lies in his throat, and thou too, and thou say'st it.

Tailor. Nay, nay, n'er be so hot, sirrah; for I fear you not. 36

San. Dost thou hear, tailor? Thou hast braved many men: brave not me. Thou'st faced many men—

Tailor. Well, sir.

San. Face not me: I'll neither be faced nor braved at thy hands, I can tell thee!

Kate. Come, come, I like the fashion of it well enough:
Here's more ado than needs; I'll have it, I;
And if you do not like it, hide your eyes. 44
I think I shall have nothing by your will.

Feran. Go, I say, and take it up for your master's use.

San. Souns, villain, not for thy life; touch it not! 48
Souns, take up my mistress' gown to his master's use!
Feran. Well, sir, what's your conceit of it?
San. I have a deeper conceit in it than you think for.
Take up my mistress' gown to his master's use! 52
Feran. Tailor, come hither; for this time take it
Hence again, and I'll content thee for thy pains.
Tailor. I thank you, sir.

[*Exit* Tailor.

Feran. Come, Kate, we now will go see thy father's
house, 56
Even in these honest mean habiliments;
Our purses shall be rich, our garments plain,
To shroud our bodies from the winter rage,
And that's enough; what should we care for more? 60
Thy sisters, Kate, to-morrow must be wed,
And I have promised them thou should'st be there:
The morning is well up; let's haste away:
It will be nine o'clock ere we come there. 64
Kate. Nine o'clock? why, 'tis already past two
In the afternoon by all the clocks in the town!
Feran. I say 'tis but nine o'clock in the morning.
Kate. I say 'tis two o'clock in the afternoon. 68
Feran. It shall be nine then ere we go to your father's:
Come back again, we will not go to-day.
Nothing but crossing of me still!
I'll have you say as I do ere you go. 72

[*Exeunt Omnes.*

[Scene VI.—*A room in* Alfonso's *house.*]

Enter Polidor, Emelia, Aurelius *and* Philema.

Pol. Fair Emelia, summer's sun-bright queen,
Brighter of hue than is the burning clime,
Where Phœbus in his bright equator sits,
Creating gold and precious minerals. 4
What would Emelia do, if I were forced
To leave fair Athens and to range the world?
Em. Should thou assay to scale the seat of Jove,
Mounting the subtle airy regions, 8
Or be snatched up as erst was Ganymede,
Love should give wings unto my swift desires,
And prune my thoughts that I would follow thee,
Or fall and perish as did Icarus. 12
Aurel. Sweetly resolvèd, fair Emelia!
But would Philema say as much to me,
If I should ask a question now of thee;
What if the Duke of Sestos' only son, 16
Which came with me unto your father's house,
Should seek to get Philema's love from me,
And make thee duchess of that stately town,
Wouldst thou not then forsake me for his love? 20
Phile. Not for great Neptune, no, nor Jove himself,
Will Philema leave Aurelius' love;
Could he instal me empress of the world,
Or make me queen and guidress of the heavens, 24

Yet would I not exchange thy love for his ;
Thy company is poor Philema's heaven,
And without thee heaven were hell to me.
Eme. And should my love, as erst did Hercules, 28
Attempt to pass the burning vaults of hell,
I would with piteous looks and pleasing words,
As once did Orpheus with his harmony,
And ravishing sound of his melodious harp, 32
Entreat grim Pluto and of him obtain,
That thou mightest go and safe return again.
Phile. And should my love, as erst Leander did,
Attempt to swim the boiling Hellespont 36
For Hero's love, no towers of brass should hold
But I would follow thee through those raging floods
With locks dishevered and my breast all bare ;
With bended knees upon Abydos' shore 40
I would with smoky sighs and brinish tears,
Importune Neptune and the watery gods
To send a guard of silver-scalèd dolphins
With sounding Tritons to be our convoy, 44
And to transport us safe unto the shore ;
Whilst I would hang about thy lovely neck,
Redoubling kiss on kiss upon thy cheeks,
And with our pastime still the swelling waves. 48
Eme. Should Polidor, as great Achilles did,
Only employ himself to follow arms,
Like to the warlike Amazonian queen
Penthesilea, Hector's paramour, 52

Who foiled the bloody Pyrrhus, murderous Greek,
I'll thrust myself amongst the thickest throngs,
And with my utmost force assist my love.
Phile. Let Æole storm, be mild and quiet thou; 56
Let Neptune swell, be Aurelius calm and pleased:
I care not, I, betide what may betide,
Let fates and fortune do the worst they can,
I reck them not; they not discord with me, 60
Whilst that my love and I do well agree.
Aurel. Sweet Philema, beauty's mineral,
From whence the sun exhales his glorious shine,
And clad the heaven in thy reflected rays! 64
And now, my liefest love, the time draws nigh,
That Hymen mounted in his saffron robe,
Must with his torches wait upon thy train,
As Helen's brothers on the hornèd moon. 68
Now, Juno, to thy number shall I add
The fairest bride that ever merchant had.
Pol. Come, fair Emelia, the priest is gone,
And at the church your father and the rest 72
Do stay to see our marriage rites performed,
And knit in sight of heaven this Gordian knot,
That teeth of fretting time may ne'er untwist:
Then come, fair love, and gratulate with me 76
This day's content and sweet solemnity. [*Exeunt Omnes.*

Sly. *Sim, must they be married now?*
Lord. *Ay, my lord.*

ACT IV

[SCENE I.—*A country road.*]

Enter FERANDO, KATE, *and* SANDER.

Sly. *Look, Sim, the fool is come again now.*

Feran. Sirrah, go fetch our horses forth and bring them to the back gate presently.

San. I will, sir, I warrant you. 4

[*Exit* SANDER.

Feran. Come, Kate, the moon shines clear to-night, methinks.

Kate. The moon? why, husband, you are deceived;
It is the sun!

Feran. Yet again? Come back again. 8
It shall be the moon ere we come at your father's.

Kate. Why, I'll say as you say: it is the moon.

Feran. Jesus save the glorious moon!

Kate. Jesus save the glorious moon! 12

Feran. I am glad, Kate, your stomach is come down.
I know it well thou knowest it is the sun;
But I did try to see if thou would'st speak,

And cross me now, as thou hast done before: 16
And trust me, Kate, hadst thou not named the moon,
We had gone back again as sure as death.
But soft, who's this that's coming here?

Enter the DUKE OF SESTOS *alone.*

Duke. Thus all alone from Sestos am I come, 20
And left my princely court and noble train,
To come to Athens, and in this disguise,
To see what course my son Aurelius takes.
But stay, here's some, it may be, travels thither. 24
Good sir, can you direct me the way to Athens?
Feran. [*to the* Duke]. Fair lovely maid, young and affable,
More clear of hue and far more beautiful
Than precious sardonyx or purple rocks 28
Of amethysts, or glistering hyacinth!
More amiable far than is the plain
Where glist'ring Cepherus in silver bowers,
Gazeth upon the giant Andromede! 32
Sweet Kate, entertain this lovely woman.
Duke. I think the man is mad; he calls me a woman.
Kate. Fair lovely lady, bright and crystalline,
Beauteous and stately as the eye-trained bird, 36
As glorious as the morning washed with dew,
Within whose eyes she takes her dawning beams,
And golden summer sleeps upon thy cheeks;
Wrap up thy radiations in some cloud, 40

Lest that thy beauty make this stately town
Inhabitable like the burning zone
With sweet reflections of thy lovely face!

Duke. What, is she mad too? or is my shape transformed,
That both of them persuade me I am a woman;
But they are mad, sure, and therefore I'll be gone,
And leave their company for fear of harm,
And unto Athens haste, to seek my son. 48

[*Exit* DUKE

Feran. Why, so, Kate; this was friendly done of thee,
And kindly, too; why, thus must we two live,
One mind, one heart, and one content for both!
This good old man does think that we are mad, 52
And glad he is, I am sure, that he is gone,
But come, sweet Kate, for we will after him,
And now persuade him to his shape again.

[*Exeunt Omnes.*

[SCENE II.—*Athens: a public place.*]

Enter ALFONSO, PHYLOTUS, VALERIA, POLIDOR, EMELIA, AURELIUS, *and* PHILEMA.

Alfon. Come, lovely sons, your marriage rites performed,
Let's hie us home to see what cheer we have;
I wonder that Ferando and his wife
Come not to see this great solemnity. 4

Pol. No marvel if Ferando be away;
His wife, I think, hath troubled so his wits,
That he remains at home to keep them warm;
For forward wedlock, as the proverb says, 8
Hath brought him to his nightcap long ago.
Phylo. But, Polidor, let my son and you take heed,
That Ferando say not ere long as much to you.
And now, Alfonso, more to show my love, 12
If unto Sestos you do send your ships,
Myself will fraught them with Arabian silks,
Rich Afric spices, Arras counter-poins,
Musk, cassia, sweet-smelling ambergris, 16
Pearl, coral, crystal, jet, and ivory,
To gratulate the favours of my son,
And friendly love that you have shown to him.
Val. And for to honour him, and this fair bride, 20

Enter the Duke of Sestos.

I'll yearly send you from my father's court,
Chests of refinèd sugar severally,
Ten tun of Tunis wine, sucket, sweet drugs,
To celebrate and solemnise this day; 24
And custom-free your merchants shall converse
And interchange the profits of your land,
Sending you gold for brass, silver for lead,
Cases of silk for packs of wool and cloth, 28
To bind this friendship and confirm this league.

Duke. I am glad, sir, that you would be so frank.
Are you become the Duke of Sestos' son,
And revel with my treasure in this town? 32
Base villain, that thou dishonourest me!

Val. [*aside*]. Souns, it is the Duke; what shall I do?—
Dishonour thee, why, know'st thou what thou say'st?

Duke. Here's no villain! He will not know me now! 36
But what say you? have you forgot me, too?

Phylo. Why, sir, are you acquainted with my son?

Duke. With thy son? No, trust me, if he be thine;
I pray you, sir, who am I? 40

Aurel. Pardon me, father! Humbly on my knees,
I do entreat your grace to hear me speak.

Duke. Peace, villain!—Lay hands on them,
And send them to prison straight. 44

[PHYLOTUS *and* VALERIA *run away.*

[*Then* SLY *speaks.*

Sly. *I say we'll have no sending to prison.*

Lord. *My lord, this is but the play; they're but in jest.*

Sly. *I tell thee, Sim, we'll have no sending to prison, that's flat. Why, Sim, am not I Don Christo Vary? Therefore, I say, they shall not go to prison.*

Lord. *No more they shall not, my lord: they be run away.*

Sly. *Are they run away, Sim? That's well; then gi's some more drink, and let them play again.* 52

Lord. *Here, my lord!*

[*Sly* drinks and then falls asleep.

Duke. Ah, treacherous boy, that durst presume
To wed thyself without thy father's leave!
I swear by fair Cynthia's burning rays, 56
By Merops' head, and by seven-mouthèd Nile,
Had I but known, ere thou hadst wedded her,
Were in thy breast the world's immortal soul,
This angry sword should rip thy hateful chest, 60
And hewed thee smaller than the Lybian sands,
Turn hence thy face, oh, cruel, impious boy!
Alfonso, I did not think you would presume
To match your daughter with my princely house, 64
And ne'er make me acquainted with the cause.
Alfon. My lord, by heavens I swear unto your grace,
I knew none other but Valeria, your man,
Had been the Duke of Sestos' noble son; 68
Nor did my daughter, I dare swear for her.
Duke. That damnèd villain that hath deluded me,
Whom I did send [for] guide unto my son!
Oh that my furious force could cleave the earth, 72
That I might muster bands of hellish fiends,
To rack his heart and tear his impious soul;
The ceaseless turning of celestial orbs
Kindles not greater flames in flitting air, 76
Than passionate anguish of my raging breast.
Aurel. Then let my death, sweet father, end your grief;
For I it is that thus have wrought your woes:
Then be revenged on me, for here I swear 80
That they are innocent of what I did.

Oh, had I charge to cut off Hydra's head,
To make the topless Alps a champion field,
To kill untamèd monsters with my sword, 84
To travail daily in the hottest sun,
And watch in winter when the nights be cold,
I would with gladness undertake them all
And think the pain but pleasure that I felt, 88
So that my noble father at my return
Would but forget and pardon my offence!

Phile. Let me entreat your grace upon my knees,
To pardon him and let my death discharge 92
The heavy wrath your grace hath vowed 'gainst him.

Pol. And, good my lord, let us entreat your grace
To purge your stomach of this melancholy:
Taint not your princely mind with grief, my lord, 96
But pardon and forgive these lovers' faults,
That kneeling crave your gracious favour here.

Eme. Great prince of Sestos, let a woman's words
Entreat a pardon in your lordly breast, 100
Both for your princely son, and us, my lord.

Duke. Aurelius, stand up; I pardon thee;
I see that virtue will have enemies,
And fortune will be thwarting honour still. 104
And you, fair virgin, too, I am content
To accept you for my daughter, since 'tis done,
And see you princely used in Sestos' court.

Phile. Thanks, good my lord, and I no longer live 108
Than I obey and honour you in all.

Alfon. Let me give thanks unto your royal grace
For this great honour done to me and mine;
And if your grace will walk unto my house, 112
I will, in humblest manner I can, show
The eternal service I do owe your grace.

Duke. Thanks, good Alfonso, but I came alone,
And not as did beseem the Sestian Duke; 116
Nor would I have it known within the town,
That I was here and thus without my train:
But as I came alone so will I go,
And leave my son to solemnise his feast; 120
And ere't be long I'll come again to you,
And do him honour as beseems the son
Of mighty Jerobel, the Sestian Duke,
Till when I'll leave you. Farewell, Aurelius! 124

Aurel. Not yet, my lord; I'll bring you to your ship.
[*Exeunt Omnes.*

[*Sly* sleeps.

Lord. *Who's within there? Come hither, sirs, my lord's*
Asleep again: go, take him easily up,
And put him in his own apparel again, 128
And lay him in the place where we did find him,
Just underneath the alehouse side below:
But see you wake him not in any case.

Boy. *It shall be done, my lord. Come, help to bear him hence.*
[Exeunt with *Sly*.

ACT V

[Scene I.—*A Room in* Alfonso's *House*.]

Enter Ferando, Aurelius, Polidor *and his* Boy, Valeria, *and* Sander.

Feran. Come, gentlemen, now that supper 's done,
How shall we spend the time till we go to bed?
Aurel. Faith, if you will, in trial of our wives,
Who will come soonest at their husband's call. 4
Pol. Nay, then Ferando he must needs sit out;
For he may call, I think, till he be weary,
Before his wife will come before she list.
Feran. 'Tis well for you that have such gentle wives, 8
Yet in this trial will I not sit out;
It may be Kate will come as soon as yours.
Aurel. My wife comes soonest, for a hundred pound.
Pol. I take it. I'll lay as much to yours, 12
That my wife comes as soon as I do send.
Aurel. How now, Ferando; you dare not lay, belike?
Feran. Why, true, I dare not lay indeed—but how?—
So little money on so sure a thing. 16
A hundred pound! why, I have laid as much

Upon my dog, in running at a deer.
She shall not come so far for such a trifle.
But will you lay five hundred marks with me, 20
And whose wife soonest comes when he doth call,
And shows herself most loving unto him,
Let him enjoy the wager I have laid?
Now, what say you? dare you adventure thus? 24
Pol. Ay, were it a thousand pounds, I durst presume
On my wife's love, and I will lay with thee.

Enter ALFONSO.

Alfon. How now, sons? What, in conference so hard?
May I, without offence, know whereabouts? 28
Aurel. Faith, father, a weighty cause about our wives,
Five hundred marks already we have laid;
And he whose wife doth show most love to him,
He must enjoy the wager to himself. 32
Alfon. Why, then, Ferando, he is sure to lose!
I promise thee, son, thy wife will hardly come,
And therefore I would not wish thee lay so much.
Feran. Tush, father, were it ten times more, 36
I durst adventure on my lovely Kate;
But if I lose, I'll pay; and so shall you.
Aurel. Upon mine honour, if I lose, I'll pay.
Pol. And so will I; upon my faith, I vow. 40
Feran. Then sit we down and let us send for them.
Alfon. I promise thee, Ferando, I am afraid thou wilt lose.

Aurel. I'll send for my wife first. Valeria,
Go bid your mistress come to me. 44
Val. I will, my lord. [*Exit* VALERIA.
Aurel. Now for my hundred pound!
Would any lay ten hundred more with me,
I know I should obtain it by her love. 48
Feran. I pray God you have not laid too much already.
Aurel. Trust me, Ferando, I am sure you have;
For you, I dare presume, have lost it all.

Enter VALERIA *again.*

Now, sirrah, what says your mistress? 52
Val. She is something busy, but she'll come anon.
Feran. Why, so. Did I not tell thee this before?
She is busy and cannot come.
Aurel. I pray God your wife send you so good an answer!
She may be busy, yet she says she'll come.
Feran. Well, well! Polidor, send you for your wife.
Pol. Agreed! Boy, desire your mistress to come hither.
Boy. I will, sir. 60
[*Exit* Boy.
Feran. Ay, so, so, he desires her to come.
Alfon. Polidor, I dare presume for thee,
I think thy wife will not deny to come:
And I do marvel much, Aurelius, 64
That your wife came not when you sent for her.

Enter the Boy *again.*

Pol. Now where's your mistress?
Boy. She bade me tell you that she will not come:
And you have any business, you must come to her. 68
Feran. Oh, monstrous, intolerable presumption,
Worse than a blazing star, or snow at midsummer,
Earthquakes or anything unseasonable!
She will not come; but he must come to her. 72
Pol. Well, sir, I pray you, let's hear what answer
Your wife will make.
Feran. Sirrah,
Command your mistress to come to me presently. 76
[*Exit* SANDER.
Aurel. I think my wife, for all she did not come,
Will prove most kind, for now I have no fear;
For I am sure Ferando's wife she will not come.
Feran. The more's the pity; then I must lose. 80

Enter KATE *and* SANDER.

But I have won, for see where Kate doth come!
Kate. Sweet husband, did you send for me?
Feran. I did, my love, I sent for thee to come:
Come hither, Kate, what's that upon thy head? 84
Kate. Nothing, husband, but my cap, I think.
Feran. Pull it off, and tread it under thy feet:
'Tis foolish; I will not have thee wear it.
[*She takes off her cap and treads on it.*

Pol. Oh, wonderful metamorphosis! 88
Aurel. This is a wonder almost past belief!
Feran. This is a token of her true love to me;
And yet I'll try her further; you shall see;
Come hither, Kate, where are thy sisters? 92
Kate. They be sitting in the bridal chamber.
Feran. Fetch them hither; and if they will not come,
Bring them perforce and make them come with thee.
Kate. I will. [*Exit.*
Alfon. I promise thee, Ferando, I would have sworn 96
Thy wife would ne'er have done so much for thee.
Feran. But you shall see she will do more than this;
For see where she brings her sisters forth by force!

Enter KATE *thrusting* PHILEMA *and* EMELIA *before her, and makes them come unto their husbands' call.*

Kate. See, husband, I have brought them both. 100
Feran. 'Tis well done, Kate.
Eme. Ay, sure, and like a loving piece; you're worthy
To have great praise for this attempt.
Phile. Ay, for making a fool of herself and us. 104
Aurel. Beshrew thee, Philema, thou hast lost me
A hundred pound to-night;
For I did lay that thou wouldst first have come.
Pol. But thou, Emelia, hast lost me a great deal more. 108
Eme. You might have kept it better then;
Who bade you lay?

Feran. Now, lovely Kate, before their husbands here,
I prithee tell unto these headstrong women 112
What duty wives do owe unto their husbands.
Kate. Then you that live thus by your pampered wills,
Now list to me and mark what I shall say:
Th' eternal power that with his only breath, 116
Shall cause this end and this beginning frame,
Not in time, nor before time, but with time, confused;—
For all the course of years, of ages, months,
Of seasons temperate, of days and hours, 120
Are tuned and stopped by measure of his hand;—
The first world was a form without a form,
A heap confused, a mixture all deformed,
A gulf of gulfs, a body bodiless, 124
Where all the elements were orderless,
Before the great Commander of the world,
The King of kings, the glorious God of heaven,
Who in six days did frame His heavenly work 128
And made all things to stand in perfect course:
Then to His image did He make a man,
Old Adam, and from his side asleep
A rib was taken, of which the Lord did make 132
The woe of man, so termed by Adam then
'Wo-man,' for that by her came sin to us;
And for her sin was Adam doomed to die.
As Sarah to her husband, so should we 136
Obey them, love them, keep, and nourish them,
If they by any means do want our helps;

Laying our hands under their feet to tread,
If that by that we might procure their ease; 140
And for a precedent I'll first begin
And lay my hand under my husband's feet.

[*She lays her hand under her husband's feet.*

Feran. Enough, sweet, the wager thou hast won;
And they, I am sure, cannot deny the same. 144

Alfon. Ay, Fernando, the wager thou hast won:
And for to show thee how I am pleased in this,
A hundred pounds I freely give thee more,
Another dowry for another daughter, 148
For she is not the same she was before.

Feran. Thanks, sweet father; gentlemen, good-night;
For Kate and I will leave you for to-night:
'Tis Kate and I am wed, and you are sped: 152
And so, farewell, for we will to our beds.

[*Exeunt* FERANDO, KATE, *and* SANDER.

Alfon. Now, Aurelius, what say you to this?

Aurel. Believe me, father, I rejoice to see
Ferando and his wife so lovingly agree. 156

[*Exeunt* AURELIUS, PHILEMA, ALFONSO, *and* VALERIA.

Eme. How now, Polidor, in a dump? What say'st thou, man?

Pol. I say thou art a shrew.

Eme. That's better than a sheep. 160

Pol. Well, since 'tis done, let it go! Come, let's in.

[*Exeunt* POLIDOR *and* EMELIA.

[EPILOGUE]

Then enter two bearing of *Sly* in his own apparel again, and leave him where they found him, and then go out. Then enter the *Tapster.*

Tapster. *Now that the darksome night is overpassed,*
And dawning day appears in crystal sky,
Now must I haste abroad. But soft, who's this?
What, Sly? oh wondrous, hath he lain here all night? 4
I'll wake him; I think he's starved by this,
But that his belly was so stuffed with ale.
What, how, Sly! Awake for shame!

Sly. *Gi's some more wine! What's all the players gone? am not I a lord?*

Tapster. *A lord, with a murrain! Come, art thou drunken still?*

Sly. *Who's this? Tapster? Oh, lord, sirrah, I have had* 12
The bravest dream to-night, that ever thou
Heardest in all thy life!

Tapster. *Ay, marry, but you had best get you home,*
For your wife will course you for dreaming here to-night. 16

Sly. *Will she? I know now how to tame a shrew!*
I dreamt upon it all this night till now,

And thou hast waked me out of the best dream
That ever I had in my life. 20
But I'll to my wife presently
And tame her too, and if she anger me.
Tapster. *Nay, tarry, Sly, for I'll go home with thee,*
And hear the rest that thou hast dreamt to-night. 24
[Exeunt Omnes.

FINIS.

TEXTUAL NOTES

AS explained more fully in the *Introduction*, the text followed, except in a few cases, is that of the Quarto of 1594, which is henceforward referred to as A. In these Notes I record all variants, except merely of spelling, found in the Quartos of 1596 and 1607, henceforward referred to as B. and C. I have also indicated all changes in the arrangement of the lines, such as the substitution of prose for verse, or the transference of a word or words to a different line. In the Stage-directions, however, *Exit* has been silently altered to *Exeunt* before two or more names.

As the spelling of the text has been modernised, I have further recorded the original form of all words in A. which seemed sufficiently noteworthy.

Among the general characteristics of the spelling in A. which have disappeared in the modernised text are (1) the frequency of silent *e* at the end of words, *e.g.*, *drinke*, *looke*, *feare*, *againe;* (2) the reduplication of letters, especially vowels, *e.g.*, *doo*, *heere*, *yoong*, *peece*, *uppe*, *farre*; the frequent use of *es* in the plural of nouns and 3rd personal singular of verbs, *e.g.*, *garmentes*, *fellowes*, *sleepes*, *weepes;* (4) the constant preference for final *ie* over *y*, *e.g.*, *Slie*, *skie*, *maie;* (5) the use of final *de* or *t* instead of *ed* in the past tense and participle, except where *ed* is sounded, *e.g.*, *promisde*, *filde*, *fecht*, *talkd*, *drest;* (6) the use of the following forms: *hir* = her; *heele*, *sheele* = he'll, she'll; *then* = than.

Ind. I. s. D., drunk. A. Droonken.

2. paunch. A. panch.

4-8. *Printed in* A. *and* B. *in doggerel verse, and divided,* anon / you / *bene* / say / heere / lying. C. *has the same arrangement, except that it prints* Omne bene *as if it were a stage-direction.*

4. feeze. A. fese.

6. instigation. A. Instegation.

7. cushion. A. cushin.

10. drizzling. A. drisling.

13. crystal. A. christall.

15. couple. A. cupple.

19. what he dooth. C. what dooeth.

20-2. *Printed in doggerel verse in* Qq. *and divided,* sleepe / bodie / furder.

24. sirrah. A. sirha. *So passim.*

28. board. A. boord.

be. *Omitted in* B. and C.

48. suits. A. sutes.

58-64. *Printed in doggerel verse in* Qq. *and divided,* Tragicall / will / . . . / shrew / men.

60. thou'lt. A. and B. thout ; C. thou'lt.

79. dandle. A. and B. dandell ; C. handle.

82. as soon. A. assoone.

88. vinegar. A. vinegre.

88. devil roar. A. divell rore.

Ind. II. *Printed in doggerel verse in* Qq. *and divided,* lord / it / board / presently.

2. A. and B. is ready; C. are ready.
3. board. A. boord.
6. Ay. A. and B. I; C. Yea.
8. erst. A. earst.
10. g'is. A. and B. gis; C. gives.
17. A. and B. fetch you; C. fetch your.
the. *Omitted in* B. and C.
23. coupled. A. cuppeld.
24. roe. A. Row.
25. tiger. A. Tygre.
28. A. and it please; B. and C. and if it please.
29. C. *has* Sim *instead of the first* Simon. *But probably* Sim *should be read instead of the second* Simon. Sly *henceforth always addresses the lord as* Sim.
29-30. *Printed in doggerel verse in* Qq. *and divided,* Simon / pot.
32. Ay. A. I. *And passim.*
33. mourned. A. moorned.
44-5. *Printed in doggerel verse in* Qq. *and divided,* bread / Sim.
44. piece. A. peece.
47-8. *Printed in doggerel verse in* Qq. *and divided,* come / plaie.
59. coats. A. cotes. *And passim.*

Act I., 1. 2. schools. C. schoole.
3. Sestos. A. Cestus. *And passim.*
11. renowned. A. renowmed.

18. scholar's. A. schollers.

21. heart. A. hart.

21. S. D., *Enter* ALFONSO, etc. Qq. Enter *Simon*, *Alphonsus*, etc. I have omitted *Simon*, as this personage is nowhere mentioned but here, and I believe the name is introduced in mistake. See further reference in *Introduction*. As *Alphonsus* occurs only here, I have substituted *Alfonso*, which is used everywhere else.

22. hue. A. hew.

24. precious. A. pretious. *And passim.*

28. quay. A. key.

29. S. D., *Exeunt* ALFONSO *and his three daughters.* Qq. *Exeunt Omnes.* But Polidor and Aurelius, with their servants, evidently remain on the stage.

40. youngest. A. yoongest. *And passim.*

50. fretted. A. fettred; B. and C. frethed. *The reading of the later* Qq. *here is preferable.*

52. scold. A. skould.

60. advice. A. advise.

63. sum. A. somme.

65. choice. A. choise.

67. A. and find; B. and C. to find.

71. A. him take; B. and C. him to take.

72. A. and B. with him; C. to him.

75. sharp of tongue. A. sharpe of toong; B. and C. sharpe in tongue.

81. centre. A. center; B. and C. censer.

84. died. A. dide.

87. merchants. A. marchants. *And passim.*

88. traffic. A. traffike.

92. A. and B. my love; C. thy love.

99. S. D., SANDER. A. SAUNDERS. A. has the three forms: *Saunders*, *Saunder*, and *Sander*, but always prefixes *San.* to his speeches. I have therefore used *Sander* throughout. This is the uniform spelling of C.

99. S. D., blue. A. blew.

105. master. A. master. *And passim.*
and. A. &; B. and C. and.
counsel. A. councell.

109. vein. A. vaine.

110. woo. A. woe.

112. gear. A. geere.

114. bonny. A. bonie.

115. venture. A. venter.

120. to't. A. toot; C. too't.

121. yield. A. yeeld.

128. our hearts. A. and B. our heartes; C. my heart.

131. you're. A. your; C. y'are.

150. gross. A. grose.

156. reach. A. reech.

160. says. A. and B. saies; *omitted in* C.

161. She's. A. Shees; C. Shee's.

175. A. your wedding day; B. and C. our wedding day.

182. so sad. Qq. *print these words at the beginning of the next line.*

186-255. *The whole of the dialogue between Sander and*

Ferando, and Sander and Polidor's boy, is printed in the Qq. *in doggerel verse, except that* C. *has* ll. 186-8 (Sander . . . while) *and* 232-4 *in prose.*

190. A. and B. didst ; C. doost.
193. wooed. A. woode.
on. *Omitted in* C.
200. she'll. A. sheele.
206. A. and B. am I ; C. I am.
216. A. and B. takes ; C. take.
219. A. a late ; B. and C. of late.
225. thumb. A. thum.
226. know. A. kno.
259. mold. A. mould.
260. A. terean plant ; C. terrene plant.
272. suddenly. A. suddainlie.
280. musician. A. Musition.
289. steal abroad. A. steele abrode.
293. agrees. A. agreese ; C. agrees.
294. doubt. A. doute.
scarce. A. skarse.
scholar. A. skoller.
You're. A. and B. Your ; C. Y'are.
303. afford. A. aforde.
308. Satins. A. Sattens.
309. fiery. A. firie.
312. too. A. and B. to ; *omitted in* C.

Act II., 1. 5. A. and B. she whom ; C. she to whome.

13. pestilence. A. pestlence.

19. You're. A. and B. Your; C. Y'are. *So also in* ll. 28 *and* 29.

24. Ay. A. and B. I; C. Yea.

28. Jack Sauce. A. jacksause.

31. foolish. *Omitted in* C.

33. Ay. A. and B. I; C. Yea.

37. A. and B. play upon; C. play on.

39. ne'er. A. neare.

41. his self. A. and B. his selfe; C. himselfe.

46. S. D., PHILEMA. Qq. *Philena.* But as they usually have the spelling *Philema*, I have adopted this throughout.

47. where's. A. whear's.

50. by'r. A. ber. *And passim.*

68. pierceth. A. pearseth.

92. sister. A. *prints this word at the beginning of the next line.*

108. Good morrow. A. godmorow.

110. Ay. A. and B. I; C. Yea.

119. A. and B. am; C. are.

121. A. and B. was; C. were.

124. A. and B. let us; C. lets.

127. wear. A. were.

135. go'st. A. goste.

139. see. A. se.

148. Kate, lovelier. A. Kate the lovelier; B. and C. Kate, thou lovelier. See *Appendix I.*, (10).

149. Apennines. A. Apenis.

150. grows. A. groes.

152. radiant. A. Raidente.

153. Xanthus. A. Zanthus.

154. Simois. A. Simies.

157. fetched. A. fecht.

159. Ploughs. A. Plous.

furrows. A. sorrowes (*misprint for* forrowes); C. furrowes.

162, 164. S. D., Exit . . . Exeunt Omnes. A. *prints in error* Exeunt Omnes *after* Ferando's *speech, and* Exit *after* Alfonso's.

Act II., II., 1-53. *The dialogue between Polidor's boy and Sander is printed in the* Qq. *in doggerel verse.*

3. You have many boys. See *Appendix I.*, (13).

16. there's. A. thears.

18. venison. A. venson.

25. warrant. A. warent.

39. imperfectious. A. imperfecksious; B. and C. imperfectious.

43. supernodical fool. A. supernodicall foule.

46. A. Here, here; B. and C. Here.

50. A. and B. words hath; C. words have.

50-1. allayed my choler. A. alaid my coller.

61-75. *The dialogue between Ferando and Sander is printed in the* Qq. *in doggerel verse.*

65. I'll. A. and B. Ile; C. I wil.

67. Sixpence. A. 6 pence.

68. Saddle. A. saddell.
72. door. A. dore.
90. leaves. A. leves.
94. A. and B. as well; C. aswel.
    matched. A. macht.
99. A. and B. doth; C. doe.
103. grown. A. grone.
107. A. and B. this two; C. these two.
114. guess. A. gesse.
119. A. and B. of what worth; C. of that worth.
120. leave. A. leve.

In the 1607 Q. *in the Bodleian* Malone *has added* to *before* censure *in MS. This emendation is probably correct.*

Act III., I., 1-20. *The dialogue between Sander, Tom, and Will is printed in the* Qq. *in doggerel verse.*

3. ready. A. redy.
5. plaguey. A. plagie.
6. Ay. A. and B. I; C. Yea.
6-7. A. and B. and thou; C. and if thou.
7. ado. A. a doo.
9. does. A. and B. dos; C. doth.
13. A. and B. wilt; C. wouldst.
14. laughing. A. laffing.
    e'en. A. ene.
17. ready. A. reddy.
20. all ready. A. and B. all redy; C. already.
22. board. A. borde.

25. adsum. A. ad sum.

26-9. *Printed in* Qq. *in doggerel verse and divided,* nose / please / villain / againe.

30. scorched. A. skorcht.

31. S. D., beats them. A. and B. beates them; C. beates them all.

32. you. *Omitted in* C.

37-8. *Printed in doggerel verse and divided,* Masters / maried *in* A. *and* B.; *arranged as prose in* C.

39-40. *Printed in doggerel verse and divided,* Sander / bootes *in* Qq.

39. laughed. A. laft.
off. A. of.

50. A. and B. As were; C. As was.

Act III., II., 15. therewithal. A. there with all.
23. ere long. A. erelong.
28. does. A. and B. dos; C. doth.

Act III., III., 1-29. *Printed in* Qq. *in doggerel verse.*
9. piece of beef. A. peese of beeffe.
24. sauciness. A. sawsinesse.
25. murrain. A. murrin.
26. A. and B. this two; C. these two.
28. A. and B. prates; C. prate.
S. D., A. and B. daggers; C. dagger.
32-3. *Divided in* Qq., shal be / have.

37-40. *Printed in* Qq. *in doggerel verse, and divided,* her / is / eate / selfe.

45. unto thy teeth. A. unto the thy teeth (*where* the *is inserted in error*); B. and C. unto thy teeth.

48. you're. A. and B. you'r; C y'are.

before. *Printed in* Qq. *at beginning of next line.*

Act III., IV., 4. A. and B. dwells in; C. dwels at.

12. Signor. A. Senior.

17. A. and B. those matters; C. these matters.

27. A. and B. state; C. estate.

50. Whenas. A. and B. When as; C. When.

Act III., V., 1-2. *Printed in* Qq. *in doggerel verse and divided,* my / here.

S. D. Enter the Haberdasher. *Added by Editor.*

5. spoke. A. spoake.

6-7. *Printed in* Qq. *in doggerel verse and divided,* give me / fit me.

S. D., on her. A. one hir.

11. meane. *Printed in* Qq. *at beginning of next line.*

14. curtailed. A. curtald.

15. be gone. A. begon.

S. D. Exit Haberdasher. *Added by Editor.*

19. you villain. A. and B. you villaine; C. thou vilaine.

20-1. *Printed in* Qq. *in doggerel verse and divided,* direction / here.

29-41. *Printed in* Qq. *in doggerel verse.*

29. loose body's gown. A. loose bodies gowne. *See Glossary.*

30. with a bottom. A. with bottome; B. and C. with a bottome.

33. throat. A. throute.

38. faced. A. faste.

53. A. and B. take; C. make.

57. habiliments. A. abilliments.

64. nine o'clock. A. nine a clocke.

65. already. A. allreadie.

66. afternoon. A. after noone.

69. A. and B. ere we go; C. ere you go.

71. A. and B. crossing of me; C. crossing me.

72. A. and B. ere you go; C. ere I go.

Act III., vi., 1. sun-bright queen. A. sun bright Queene; B. and C. bright sun Queene.

2. hue. A. hew.

4. precious minerals. A. pressious minneralls.

5. forced. A. forst.

8. subtle airy. A. subtle ayrie.

9. snatched. A. snacht.

24. guidress. A. guidres.

25. A. thy love; B. and C. my love.

29. to pass. *Omitted in* C.
vaults. A. valtes.

36. Hellespont. A. Helispont.

40. Abydos'. A. Abidas.

49. great. *Omitted in* C.
52. paramour. A. paramore.
53. Greek. A. greeke.
56. Æole. A. Eole.
62. beauty's mineral. A. bewties mynerall.
67. wait. A. waight.
71. priest. A. preeste.

Act IV., I., 6. methinks. *Printed in* Qq. *at beginning of next line.*

9. It shall be. *Printed in* Qq. *at end of previous line.*
24. thither. A. thether.
25. direct. A. derect.
26. S. D. Feran. [to the Duke]. Qq. *have:* Ferando speakes to the olde man.
27. clear. A. cleere.
29. amethysts. A. Amithests.
hyacinth. A. Hyasinthe.
31. bowers. A. boures.
40. A. Wrap up; B. and C. Wrapt up.
53. A. and B. glad he is; C. glad is he.

Act IV., II., 4. A. Comes not; B. and C. Come not.

15. Afric. A. Affrick.
A. and B. counter poines; C. counter pointes.
16. ambergris. A. Ambergrees.
17. coral. A. curroll; B. currol; C. curtol.
19. shown. A. shone.
20. A. and B. this faire; C. this his faire.

21. yearly. A. yerly.

A. and B. my fathers; C. your fathers.

25. A. and B. converse; C. commerce.

28. wool. A. woll.

S. D., A. and B. runnes away; C. runne away.

47-8. to prison, that's flat. *Printed in* Qq. *at beginning of the next line.*

50. they be run away. *A separate line in* Qq.

61. hewed. *We should have expected* hew, *but the writer is borrowing from Marlowe.* Cf. *Appendix I.* (16).

63. Alfonso. C. *prints Alfon. as a stage direction prefixed to the line.*

64. match. A. mach.

71. send for guide. A. send guide; B. and C. send for guide. *I have adopted the reading of the later* Qq., *as metrically preferable, though* n *in send may be semi-vocalic.*

83. A. and B. champion field; C. champaine field.

85. travail. A. travell.

90. A. and B. pardon; C. pardon me.

121. be long. A. belong; B. and C. be long.

128. in his own. A. in his one; B. and C. in his own.

133. S. D. *The* Qq. *have merely* Exit.

Act V., I., 4. soonest; A. sownest.

5. A. and B. Nay then; C. then then.

10, 13. A. and B. as soone as yours; C. as soone as I do send.

15. But how. *Printed in* Qq. *at beginning of next line.*

16. money. A. mony.

22. herself. A. her selfe.

26. wife's. A. wives.

28. whereabouts. A. and B. where abouts; C. where about.

29. weighty. A. waighty.

33. A. and B. lose; C. lose it.

55. A. and B. She is busie; C. She was busie.

61. desires. A. desiers.

73. answer. *Printed in the* Qq. *at the beginning of the next line.*

75-6. *Printed in* Qq., Sirra . . . come / To . . . presentlie.

105. lost me. *Printed in* Qq. *at the beginning of the next line.*

112. headstrong. A. hedstrong.

114. pampered. A. pompered; B. and C. pampered.

116. Th' eternal. A. Theternall; B. and C. Th' eternal.

119. months. A. moneths.

129. perfect. A. perfit.

141. precedent. A. president.

143. *In the* 1607 Q. *in the Bodleian* Malone *has added* Kate *after* sweet *in MS. The emendation may be correct.*

150. good-night. A. godnight.

161. A. and B. let it go, come lets in; C. come lets go.

Epilogue, S. D., A. and B. enter the Tapster; C. enters the Tapster.

7. A. What how; B. and C. What now.

8-9. *Printed in* A. *and* B. *in doggerel verse and divided,* all the / Lord; *arranged as prose in* C.

8. Gi's. A. and B. gis; C. gives.

A. whats; B. and C. what.

12-14. *Arranged as prose in* C.

14. Heardest. A. Hardest.

15. Ay, marry. A. and B. I, marry; C. Yea mary.

20-2. *Divided in* A. *and* B., my / too / me. C. *arranges them in two lines,* presently / me.

22. A. and B. And if she; C. If she.

GLOSSARIAL INDEX

I HAVE included in this Glossarial Index (1) words or phrases which present difficulty to a modern reader; (2) words, *e.g.*, *abusious*, of which the meaning is clear, but the form unusual, or otherwise noteworthy; (3) allusions in more or less Euphuistic vein to animals, flowers, and minerals; (4) mythological, historical, and geographical references, except a few of the most familiar type. A number of the references in (4) are taken from Marlowe, and are dealt with further in *Appendix I.* and in the *Introduction.*

ABUSIOUS, abusive, II. ii. 38

ABYDOS, in Mysia, the home of Leander, III. vi. 40

ACHILLES, III. vi. 49

ADAM, V. i. 131

ADSUM, I am here, III. i. 5

ÆOLE, Æolus, god of the winds, III. vi. 56

AFFABLE, charming, IV. i. 26

AFRIC SPICES, IV. ii. 15

ALCIDES, Hercules, the grandson of Alcæus, III. i. 50

ALPS, IV. ii. 83

AMBERGRIS, an odoriferous, wax-like substance, IV. ii. 17

AMETHYSTS, IV. i. 29

AMIABLE, lovely, IV. i. 30

AND, if, Ind. i. 51. The double form 'And if' is used.

ANDROMEDE, apparently a fictitious classical allusion. From the context it seems as if the reference were to a supposed mountain, IV. i. 32.

APENNINES, II. i. 149.

ARABIAN SILKS, IV. ii. 14

ARISTOTLE, WALKS OF, I. i. 2

ARRAS COUNTER-POINS, quilted bed covers from Arras, in Artois, IV. ii. 15

BEHOLDING, beholden, III. iii. 44

Belike, apparently, probably, II. ii. 53; V. i. 14
Boreas, the north wind, II. I. 150
Bottom, skein, III. v. 30
Brainsick, mad, I. i. 167
Braved, used in the double sense of 'made fine' and 'browbeaten,' III. v. 37
Bravest, finest, Ep. 13
Bridehouse, house where a wedding is held, II. ii. 15
Brinish, briny, I. i. 5

Cæsar, I. i. 15
Canibey, an apparently fictitious geographical allusion, II. i. 74
Cassia, the bark of an aromatic tree, IV. ii. 16
Catapie, the name which Polidor's boy gives to himself, I. i. 251.
Cause, case, circumstance, IV. ii. 65
Celestial orbs, Turning of, the motion of the spheres, IV. ii. 75
Censure, judgment, II. ii. 120
Cepherus, apparently a mistake for Cephisus, a river in Attica, IV. i. 31
Champion field, a level, open field, IV. ii. 83
Chest, breast, IV. ii. 60
Chud, I would: the conventional rustic form in Elizabethan drama, I. i. 194
Circumstance, full details, I. i. 204
Comprise, carry out, attain, III. ii. 31
Conceit, idea, III. v. 50
Converse, traffic, IV. ii. 25
Course, thrash, III. iii. 17; Ep. 16
Coxcomb, head, II. i. 31
Crisee, By, an exclamation, for which I have not been able to find a parallel: it may be a corruption of "By Christ," as in "Criscross," Ind. i. 4
Cross, strike a blow across, II. i. 29
Cry, Out of all, beyond measure, I. i. 217; II. ii. 20, 27
Cunning, cleverness, skill, I. i.

Curtailed, cut short, small, III. v. 14
Curtal, a horse with docked tail, II. ii. 62
Cushion, a drinking vessel, Ind. i. 7
Cynthia, the moon, IV. ii. 56
Cytherea, Venus: her silver doves, III. ii. 6

Darksome, dark, Ind. i. 13; Ep. 1
Decorum, seemly order, discipline, III. ii. 28
Diana, Purple robe of, II. i. 198
Dishevered, used in the sense of dishevelled, III. vi. 39
Dolphins, III. vi. 43
Drift, design, III. ii. 31
Dump, doleful mood, I. i. 30; V. i.

Ecce signum, behold the proof. Sander alludes to Ferando's coat of arms on his livery, I. i. 237
Egeus, King of Thrace, III. i. 51

Exhales, draws forth, III. vi. 63

Faced, used in the double sense of "trimmed" and "threatened," III. v. 38
Feeze, drive away, beat, Ind. i. 4.
Fellows, equals, Ind. I. 37
Flatly, in downright manner, III. iii. 45
Flitting, variable, inconstant motion, IV. ii. 76
Frank, liberal, open-handed, IV. ii. 30
Fraught, freight, IV. ii. 14
Fretting, wearing away, III. vi. 75

Ganymede, III. vi. 9
Gear, business, I. i. 112
Gi's, give us, Ind. ii. 10, etc.
Gordian knot, used of marriage, III. vi. 74
Gratulate, express joy or gratitude at, Ind. ii. 33; III. vi. 76; IV. ii. 18
Guidress, a feminine form of *guider*, III. vi. 24

Hap, fate, II. i. 69

HEADMEN of the parish, a punning allusion to the "horns" of a cuckold, I. i. 200-1.
HECTOR, III. vi. 52
HELENA, Helen of Troy, I. i. 83
HELEN'S BROTHERS, Castor and Pollux, III. vi. 68
HELLESPONT, I. i. 5; II. i. 75; III. vi. 36
HERCULES, III. vi. 28
HERO, of Sestos, III. vi. 37
HOP OF MY THUMB, I. i. 225
How, an expression of surprise, Ep. 7
HYACINTH, a precious stone, IV. i. 29
HYDRA, IV. ii. 82
HYMEN, III. vi. 66

IBIS, THE GOLDEN BEAK OF, an imaginary attribute of the Egyptian deity.
ICARUS, the son of Dædalus, who, in attempting to fly, fell into the Ægean Sea, III. vi. 12
IDA, a mountain near Troy, II. i. 154
IMPERFECTIOUS, full of faults, II. ii. 39
INDIE, I. i. 309
INHABITABLE, uninhabitable, IV. i. 42
INVADE, assault, II. ii. 42
ITALIAN MERCHANTS, II. i. 158

JACK SAUCE, impudent fellow, II. i. 28
JAGS, slits in a garment, III. v. 18
JUNO, (*a*) in the Judgement of Paris, II. i. 82; (*b*) as the goddess of marriage, III. vi. 69

KINDLY, in accordance with the ties of kinship, IV. i. 50

LAMBS AND LIONS, II. i. 120
LEANDER, I. i. 4; III. vi. 35
LIEFEST, dearest, III. vi. 65
LOOSE-BODIED GOWN, used particularly of the dress of light women, and then as a term for the women themselves, III. v. 28. But there is no need to change the reading of all the Qq. in the next line, *loose bodies gowne*, though

Proverbial phrases:—
'The woodcock wants his tail,' I. i. 158
'Forward wedlock hath brought him to his night-cap,' IV. ii. 8-9
Prune, preen or trim for flight, III. vi. 11
Pyrrhus, son of Achilles, III. vi. 53

Radiations, rays, IV. i. 40
Rare, strange, wonderful, III. ii. 28
Resolve, enlighten, inform, I. i. 35
Round-compassed, cut in circular shape, III. v. 23
Russian stems, Russian ships, II. i. 158

Sarah, Abraham's wife, V. i. 136
Sardonyx, a precious stone, IV. i. 28
Sestos, in Thrace, the home of Hero, I. i. 3, etc.
Several, separate, individual, II. ii. 120
Shine, radiance, III. vi. 63
Shroud, cover, III. v. 59
Simois, a river in the Troad, II. i. 154
Slash, make slits in a garment, for the insertion of stripes of a different colour, I. i. 211
Something, somewhat, V. i. 53
Sort, fashion, II. ii. 84
Spoke for, ordered, III. v. 5
Stomach, pride, IV. i. 13
Stout, bold, I. i. 216
Sucket, a sweetmeat, IV. ii. 23
Supernodical, supreme, II. ii. 43
Swash it out, swagger, I. i. 211

Ten commandments, ten finger nails, I. i. 153
Tenedos, an island off the coast of Troy, I. i. 85
Terean plant, a fabulous plant which turns to stone, I. i. 260
Terms, Stand not on, do not stand on ceremonies, II. ii. 87
Terrene Main, Mediterranean Sea, II. i. 159

THRACIAN HORSE. Tamed by Hercules in one of his labours. III. i. 50
THUMS, beats, II. ii. 27
TILLY VALLY, an expression of contempt, Ind. i. 4
TIMBER, stuff, II. ii. 36
'TIRED, attired, II. i. 142
TRAVAIL, work, IV. ii. 85
TRITONS, sea-gods who blow through shells, III. vi. 44
TUNIS WINE, IV. ii. 23

UNDERMINE, dig beneath, II. i. 78
USE, custom, I. i. 227

WATCH, keep awake, IV. ii. 86
WAXEN, grown, II. ii. 26
WELKIN, sky, Ind. i. 12

XANTHUS, a river in the Troad, II. i. 153

APPENDIX I

Passages from Marlowe's *Tamburlaine* and *Doctor Faustus* in *The Taming of a Shrew*

In this Appendix I have made a detailed and systematic inventory of the passages borrowed either verbally or with more or less adaptation by the author of *The Taming of a Shrew* from *Tamburlaine* and *Doctor Faustus*. In drawing up the list of parallels, I have made use of the labours of the American correspondent in Knight's *Shakspere*, ii., 114-15; of Samuel Hickson in *Notes and Queries*, Vol. I., 226-7 (1850); of Dyce in *Some Account of Marlowe and his Writings* prefixed to his edition of Marlowe's *Works*; of Dr. Furnivall in his *Forewords* to C. Praetorius' Facsimile of the first Quarto of the play; of Dr. A. W. Ward in his edition of *Doctor Faustus*; of Mr. Bullen in the *Introduction* to his edition of Marlowe's *Works*; of Professor Courthope in his *History of English Poetry*, Vol. IV., Appendix, 471-2; and of Mr. R. Warwick Bond in his *Introduction* to *The Taming of the Shrew* (Arden edition). My list is, however, I believe, the fullest that has yet been made,[1] and in every case I have given the exact readings of the earliest editions of the plays, and added the names of the speakers. I have also, for purposes of reference, used the numbering of Mr. Bullen's edition. The wider aspects of the subject are treated in the *Introduction*, but I have drawn attention below to one or two textual points. It is important also to notice that

[1] It was in print before I saw the list given by Prof. Tolman in *Shakespeare's Part in the Taming of the Shrew* (Publications of Mod. Lang. Assoc. of America, Vol. V., 4), which is also very full.

in extracts I and 13 the quotations in *A Shrew* from *Doctor Faustus* represent the text of the edition of 1616 and not of 1604, except that in 13 "such pickadevantes" is used instead of "beards," and that "seene," the reading of both editions of *Doctor Faustus*, is omitted in *A Shrew*, possibly in error. Moreover, extract 16, as Ward has pointed out, only occurs in the text of 1616, and is not found in that of 1604. And I may add that the Duke's melodramatic outburst (IV., II., 72-4) about "mustering bands of hellish fiends" to torture Valeria, is doubtless inspired by the immediately following episode in the edition of 1616, where Faustus summons Mephistophiles "and other Divels" to punish his enemies. It is therefore certain that the version of *Doctor Faustus* known to the author of *A Shrew* before 1594 was more akin to the edition of 1616 than that of 1604. This is a remarkable point which has never yet been adequately taken into consideration in weighing the respective authority of the two editions It is evident that whoever may have been the writer or writers of the passages which are found only in the edition of 1616, they have far greater importance if they date, as some of them must do, from before 30th September (or 2nd October),[1] 1594, when the play was revived by the Lord Admiral's Men. Mr. Fleay's statement (Appendix A in Dr. Ward's edition of *Faustus*) that "the additions" made by Bird and Rowley, and paid for by Henslowe on 22nd November, 1602, "are certainly those contained in the 1616 edition," is proved by the above evidence to be incorrect. Bird and Rowley's additions may be contained in the 1616 text, but it certainly has also unique features that probably date from before Marlowe's death.

[1] *Cf.* Mr. Greg's *Henslowe's Diary*, Part II., under *Doctor Faustus*.

(1) INDUCTION, i., 9-12.

Lord. Now that the gloomie shaddow of the night
Longing to view Orions drisling lookes,
Leapes from th' antarticke world unto the skie
And dims the welkin with her pitchie breath.

Doctor Faustus, Sc. iii., 1-4.

Faustus. Now that the gloomy shadow of the earth, [1616 night]
Longing to view *Orions* drisling looke,
Leapes from th' antartike world unto the skie,
And dimmes the welkin with her pitchy breath.

(2) INDUCTION, ii., 19-21.

Will. Ile fetch you lustie steedes more swift of pace
Then winged *Pegasus* in all his pride,
That ran so swiftly over the Persian plaines.

1 *Tamburlaine*, I., ii., 93-4.

Tamb. A hundreth Tartars shall attend on thee
Mounted on Steeds swifter than *Pegasus*;
Thy Garments shall be made of Medean silke.

(3) ACT I., i., 22-4.

Aurel. But staie; what dames are these so bright of hew
Whose eies are brighter than the lampes of heaven,
Fairer then rocks of pearle and pretious stone?

1 *Tamburlaine*, III., iii., 117-20.

Tamb. *Zenocrate*, the loveliest Maide alive,
Fairer than rockes of pearle and pretious stone,
The onely Paragon of *Tamburlaine*,
Whose eies are brighter than the Lamps of heaven.

(4) Act I., i., 61-4.

Aurel. And yet I needs must love his second daughter,
The image of honor and Nobilitie,
In whose sweet person is comprisde the somme
Of natures skill and heavenlie majestie.

1 *Tamburlaine*, V., i., 74-9.

1 *Virgin.* Most happy King and Emperour of the earth,
Image of Honor and Nobilitie,
For whome the Powers divine have made the world,
And on whose throne the holy Graces sit;
In whose sweete person is compriz'd the Sum
Of natures Skill and heavenly majestie.

(5) Act I., i., 81-5.

Aurel. O might I see the center of my soule
Whose sacred beautie hath inchanted me,
More faire then was the Grecian *Helena*
For whose sweet sake so many princes dide
That came with thousand shippes to *Tenedos.*

2 *Tamburlaine*, II., iv., 83-9.

Tamb. . . . pale and ghastly death,
Whose darts do pierce the Center of my soule.
Her sacred beauty hath enchaunted heaven;
And had she liv'd before the siege of *Troy*,
Hellen, whose beauty sommond Greece to armes,
And drew a thousand ships to *Tenedos*,
Had not beene nam'd in *Homers* Iliads.

The extract from *Tamburlaine* proves that the reading in the quarto of 1594 of *Taming of a Shrew, the center of my soule*, is right. The two later quartos have *the censer*, etc.

(6) Act II., i., 56-9.

Pol. Come, faire *Emelia*, my lovelie love,
Brighter then the burnisht pallace of the sunne,
The eie sight of the glorious firmament,
In whose bright lookes sparkles the radiant fire.

2 *Tamburlaine*, I., iii., 1-4.

Tamb. Now, bright *Zenocrate*, the worlds faire eie,
Whose beames illuminate the lamps of heaven,
Whose chearful looks do cleare the clowdy aire,
And cloath it in a christall liverie.

(7) Act II., i., 67-9.

Emel. Eternall heaven sooner be dissolvde,
And all that pearseth Phebus' silver eie,
Before such hap befall to *Polidor*.

1 *Tamburlaine*, III., ii., 18-20.

Agydas. Eternall heaven sooner be dissolv'd,
And all that pierceth *Phoebes* silver eie,
Before such hap fall to *Zenocrate*.

A comparison of the second lines in these extracts shows that *Phœbes* is possibly the right reading in *Taming of a Shrew*, but the author may have blundered in his use of classical names.

(8) Act II., i., 79-80.

Aurel. To seeke for strange and new-found pretious stones,
And dive into the sea to gather pearle.

Doctor Faustus, Sc. i., 81-2.

Faustus. Ransacke the Ocean for orient pearle,
And search all corners of the new found world.

(9) ACT II., i., 131-2.

Feran. As was the Massie Robe that late adornd
The stately legate of the Persian King.

(*a*) 1 *Tamburlaine*, III., i., 43-4.

Basso. And show your pleasure to the Persean
As fits the Legate of the stately Turk.

(*b*) 2 *Tamburlaine*, III., ii., 123-4.

Tamb. And I sat downe cloth'd with the massie robe
That late adorn'd the Affrike Potentate.

(10) ACT II., i., 148-9.

Feran. Sweete *Kate*, the lovelier then Diana's purple robe,
Whiter then are the snowie Apenis.

(*a*) 1 *Tamburlaine*, I., ii., 87-9.

Tamb. *Zenocrate*, lovelier than the Love of *Jove*,
Brighter than is the silver Rhodolfe,
Fairer than whitest snow on Scythian hils.

A comparison of the first lines in these two extracts makes it probable that *the* before *lovelier* in *Taming of a Shrew*, II., i., 148 (changed to *thou* in the two later quartos) is printed by mistake.

(*b*) 2 *Tamburlaine*, I., i., 111.

That rests upon the snowy Apennines.

(11) ACT II., i., 151.

Feran. Father, I sweare by Ibis golden beake.

1 *Tamburlaine*, IV., iii., 35-6.

Soldan of Egypt. A sacred vow to heaven and him I make,
Confirming it with *Ibis* holy name.

(12) Act II., i., 156-9.

Ferand. Thou shalt have garments wrought of Median silke,
Enchast with pretious Jewells fecht from far,
By Italian Marchants that with Russian stemes
Plous up huge forrowes in the *Terren Maine*.

(*a*) 1 *Tamburlaine*, I., ii., 95-6.

Tamb. Thy Garments shall be made of Medean silke,
Enchast with precious jewels of mine owne.

(*b*) 1 *Tamburlaine*, I., ii., 192-93.

Tamb. And Christian Merchants, that with Russian stems
Plow up huge furrowes in the Caspian sea.

(*c*) 2 *Tamburlaine*, I., i., 37.

Orcanes. The Terrene Main wherin *Danubius* falls.

(13) Act II., ii., 1-4.

Boy. Come hither, sirha, boy.
San. Boy, oh disgrace to my person, souns, boy
Of your face, you have many boies with such
Pickadevantes I am sure, souns would you
Not have a bloudie nose for this!

Doctor Faustus, Sc. iv., 1-4.

(*a*) Edition of 1604.

Wagner. Sirra boy, come hither.

Clown. How, boy? swowns, boy, I hope you have seene many boyes with such pickadevaunts as I have. Boy quotha.

(*b*) Edition of 1616.

Wagner. Come hither, sirra boy.

Clown. Boy? O disgrace to my person: Zounds boy in your face, you have seene many boyes with beards, I am sure.

(14) ACT III., i., 49-51.

Feran. Were she as stuborne or as full of strength
As were the *Thracian* horse *Alcides* tamde,
That King *Egeus* fed with flesh of men.

2 *Tamburlaine*, IV., iv., 12-14.

Tamb. The headstrong Jades of Thrace *Alcides* tam'd,
That King *Egeus* fed with humaine flesh
And made so wanton that they knew their strengths.

(15) ACT III., vi., 31-2.

Emelia. As once did *Orpheus* with his harmony,
And ravishing sound of his melodious harpe.

Doctor Faustus, Sc. vi., 28-9.

Dr Faustus. And hath not he that built the walles of *Thebes*,
With ravishing sound of his melodious harp.

(16) ACT IV., ii., 60-1.

Duke. This angrie sword should rip thy hatefull chest,
And hewd thee smaller than the *Libian* sands.

Doctor Faustus, Sc. x.*a* (*Appendix*, p. 306).

Dr. Faustus. And had you cut my body with your swords,
Or hew'd this flesh and bones as small as sand.

APPENDIX II

THE "INDUCTION" STORY

XVIth and XVIIth Century Prose Versions

I have discussed in the *Introduction* the chief extant forms of the story of the trick played on the drunkard by the lord. I here reprint four versions dating from the latter part of the sixteenth or the earlier part of the seventeenth century.

"A," that of Heuterus, was first published in 1584. It was quoted by Warton in his *History of English Poetry*, Vol. III., pp. 294-5, and by Mr. Warwick Bond in his *Introduction* to *The Taming of the Shrew* in the "Arden" edition. The first edition of Heuterus' Chronicle is not in the British Museum, but I have compared Warton's citation with a seventeenth century edition, published in 1639.

"B" is Simon Goulart's version (probably based upon "A") as translated by Edward Grimeston in 1607. It has been reprinted in Part I., Vol. iv., of Collier's *Shakespeare's Library* (Hazlitt's edition, 1875, pp. 403-5).

"C" is the fragment of a lost work discovered by Mr. H. G. Norton, and published by him in the Shakespeare Society's Papers, 1845; it was reprinted in Part I., Vol. iv., of Collier's *Shakespeare's Library* (Hazlitt's edition,

1875, pp. 406-14). For reasons given in the *Introduction*, I believe that this version is later than "B," and does not date from 1570, as Norton supposed.

"D" was published by Sir R. Barckley, in 1598, and is thus earlier than "B" or "C," but, unlike the other versions, it makes the Emperor Charles V. the author of the trick instead of Philip the Good of Burgundy. Heuterus' Chronicle cannot then have been Barckley's source. His version has not, so far as I am aware, been reprinted.

A

From Heuterus, *De Rebus Burgundicis*, Bk. IV., p. 150

Nocte quadam a cæna cum aliquot præcipuis amicorum per urbem deambulans, jacentem conspicatus est medio foro hominem de plebe ebrium, altum stertentem. In eo visum est experiri quale esset, vitæ nostræ ludicrum, de quo illi interdum essent collocuti. Jussit hominem deferri ad Palatium, et lecto Ducali collocari, nocturnum Ducis pileum capiti ejus imponi, exutaque sordida vestilinea, aliam e tenuissimo ei lino indui. De mane ubi evigilavit, præsto fuere pueri nobiles et cubicularii Ducis, qui non aliter quam ex Duce ipso quærerent an luberet surgere, et quemadmodum vellet eo loci vestiri. Prolata sunt Ducis vestimenta. Mirari homo ubi se eo loci vidit. Indutus est, prodiit a cubiculo, adfuere proceres qui illum ad sacellum deducerent. Interfuit sacro, datus est illi osculandus liber, et reliqua penitus ut Duci. A sacro ad prandium instructissimum. A prandio cubicularius attulit chartas lusorias, pecuniæ acervum. Lusit cum magnatibus, sub serum deambulavit in hortulis, venatus est in leporario, et cepit aves aliquot aucupio. Cæna peracta est pari celebritate qua prandium. Accensis luminibus inducta sunt musica instrumenta, puellæ atque nobiles adolescentes saltarunt, exhibitæ sunt fabulæ, dehinc comessatio quæ hilaritate atque invitationibus ad potandum, producta est in multam noctem. Ille vero largiter se vino obruit præstantissimo; et postquam collapsus in somnum altissimum jussit eum Dux vestimentis prioribus indui, atque in eum locum reportari, quo prius fuerat repertus: ibi transegit noctem totam dormiens. Postridie experrectus cæpit secum de vita illa Ducali cogitare, incertum habens fuissetne res vera, an visum quod animo esset per quietem observatum. Tandem collatis conjecturis omnibus atque argumentis, statuit somnium fuisse, et ut tale uxori liberis ac viris narravit. Quid interest inter diem illius et nostros aliquot annos? Nihil penitus, nisi quod hoc est paulo diuturnius somnium, ac si quis unam duntaxat horam, alter vero decem somniasset.

B

From Edward Grimeston's Translation of S. Goulart's *Thrésor d'histoires admirables et memorables*, pp. 587-9

Vanity of the World as represented in State

Philip called the good Duke of Bourgondy, in the memory of our ancestors, being at Bruxells with his Court and walking one night after supper through the streets, accompanied with some of his favorits: he found lying upon the stones a certaine Artisan that was very dronke, and that slept soundly. It pleased the Prince in this Artisan to make triall of the vanity of our life, whereof he had before discoursed with his familiar friends. Hee therfore caused this sleeper to be taken up and carried into his Pallace: hee commands him to bee layed in one of the richest beds, a riche Night-cap to bee given him, his foule shirt to bee taken off, and to have an other put on him of fine Holland: when as this Dronkard had digested his Wine, and began to awake: behold there comes about his bed, Pages and Groomes of the Dukes Chamber, who draw the Curteines, make many courtesies, and being bare-headed, aske him if it please him to rise, and what appareil it would please him to put on that day. They bring him rich apparrell. The new Monsieur amazed at such curtesie, and doubting whether he dreampt or waked, suffered himselfe to be drest, and led out of the Chamber. There came Noblemen which saluted him with all honour, and conduct him to the Masse, where with great ceremonie they give him the Booke of the Gospell, and the Pixe to Kisse, as they did usually unto the Duke: from the Masse they bring him backe unto the Pallace: hee washes his hands, and sittes downe at the Table well furnished. After dinner, the great Chamberlaine commandes Cardes, to be brought with a great summe of money. This Duke in Imagination playes with the chiefe of the Court. Then they carrie him to walke in the Gardein, and to hunt the Hare and to Hawke. They bring him back unto the Pallace, where hee sups in state. Candles beeing light, the Musitions begin to play, and the Tables taken away, the Gentlemen and Gentle-women fell to dancing, then they played a pleasant Comedie, after which followed a Banket, whereas they had presently store of Ipocras and precious Wine, with all sorts of confitures, to this Prince of the new Impression, so as he was drunke, & fell soundlie a sleepe. Here-upon the Duke commanded that hee should bee disrobed of all his riche attire. Hee was put into his olde ragges and carried into the same place, where he had been found the night before, where hee spent that night. Being awake in the morning, hee began to remember what had happened before, hee knewe not whether it were true in deede, or a dreame that had troubled his braine. But in the end, after many discourses, hee concluds that all was but a dreame that had happened unto him, and so entertained his wife, his Children and his neighbors, without any other apprehension. This Historie put mee in minde of that which Seneca sayth in the ende of his 59 letter to Lucilius. No man, saies he, can reioyce and content himselfe, if he be not nobly minded, iust and temperate. What then? Are the wicked deprived of all ioye? they are glad as the Lions that have found their prey. Being full of wine and luxury, having spent the night in gourmandise, when as pleasures poored into this vessell of the bodie (beeing to little to containe so much) beganne to foame out, these miserable wretches crie with him of whome Virgill speakes,

Thou knowest, how in the midest of pastimes false & vaine,
We cast and past our latest night of paine.

The dissolute spend the night, yea the last night in false ioyes. O man, this stately usage of the above named Artisan, is like unto a dreame that passeth. And his goodly day, and the years of a wicked life differ nothing but in more and lesse. He slept foure and twenty houres, other wicked men some-times foure and twenty thousands of houres. It is a little or a great dreame: and nothing more.

C

The Waking Man's Dreame

The Fifth Event

The Greeke proverbe saith that a man is but the dreame of a shaddow, or the shaddow of a dreame: is there then anything more vaine then a shadow, which is nothing in it selfe, being but a privation of light framed by the opposition of a thicke body unto a luminous? is there any thing more frivolous then a dreame, which hath no subsistence but in the hollownesse of a sleeping braine, and which, to speake properly, is nothing but a meere gathering together of Chimericall Images, and this is it which makes an ancient say, that we are but dust and shadow: our life is compared unto those, who sleeping dreame that they eate, and waking find themselves empty and hungry; and who is he that doth not find this experimented in himselfe, as often as he revolves in his memory the time which is past? Who can in these passages of this world distinguish the things which have been done from those that have been dreamed? vanities, delights, riches, pleasures and all are past and gone; are they not dreames? What hath our pride and pompe availed us? say those poore miserable soules shut up in the infernall prisons: where is our bravery become, and the glorious show of our magnificence? all these things are passed like a flying shadow, or as a post who hastens to his journeyes end. This is it which caused the ancient Comicke Poet to say that the world was nothing but an universall Comedy, because all the passages thereof serve but to make the wisest laugh: and according to the opinion of Democritus, all that is acted in this great Theater of the whole world, when it is ended, differs in nothing from what hath bin acted on a Players stage: the mirrour which I will heere set before your eyes will so lively expresse all these verities, and so truly shew the vanities of all the greatnesse and opulencies of the earth, that although in these Events, I gather not either examples not farre distant from our times, or that have beene published by any other writer, yet I beleeve that the serious pleasantnesse of this one will supply its want of novelty, and that its repetition will neither bee unfruitfull nor unpleasing.

In the time that Phillip Duke of Burgundy (who by the gentlenesse and curteousnesse of his carriage purchaste the name of good) guided the reines of the country of Flanders, this prince, who was of an humour pleasing, and full of judicious goodnesse, rather then silly simplicity, used pastimes which for their singularity are commonly called the pleasures of Princes: after this manner he no lesse shewed the quaintnesse of his wit then his prudence.

Being in Bruxelles with all his court, and having at his table discoursed amply enough of the vanities and greatnesse of this world, he let each one say his pleasure on this subject, whereon was alleadged grave sentences and rare examples: walking towards the evening in the towne, his head full of divers thoughts, he found a Tradesman lying in a corner sleeping very soundly, the fumes of Bacchus having surcharged his braine. I describe this mans drunkenesse in as good manner as I can to the credit of the party. This vice is so common in both the superior and inferiour German, that divers, making glory and vaunting of their dexterity in this art, encrease their praise thereby, and hold it for a brave act. The good Duke, to give his followers an example of the vanity of all the magnificence with which he was invironed, devised a meanes farre lesse dangerous than that which Dionysius the Tyrant used towards Democles, and which in pleasantnesse beares a marvellous utility. He caused his men to carry away this sleeper, with whom, as with a blocke, they might doe what they would, without awaking him; he caused them to carry him into one of the sumptuosest parts of his Pallace, into a chamber most statelike furnished, and makes them lay him on a rich bed. They presently strip him of his bad cloathes, and put him on a very fine and cleane shirt, instead of his own, which was foule and filthy. They let him sleepe in that place at his ease, and whilest hee settles his drinke the Duke prepares the pleasantest pastime that can be imagined.

In the morning, this drunkard being awake drawes the curtaines of this brave rich bed, sees himselfe in a chamber adorned like a Paradice, he considers the rich furniture with an amazement such as you may imagine: he beleeves not his eyes, but layes his fingers on them, and feeling them open, yet perswades himselfe they are shut by sleep, and that all he sees is but a pure dreame.

As soone as he was knowne to be awake, in comes the officers of the Dukes house, who were instructed by the Duke what they should do. There were pages bravely apparelled, Gentlemen of the chamber, Gentleman waiters, and the High Chamberlaine, who, all in faire order, and without laughing bring cloathing for this new guest; they honour him with the same great reverences as if he were a Soveraigne Prince; they serve him bare headed, and aske him what suite he will please to weare that day.

This fellow, affrighted at the first, believing these things to be inchantment or dreames, reclaimed by these submissions, tooke heart, and grew bold, and setting a good face on the matter, chused amongst all the apparell that they presented unto him that which he liked best, and which hee thought to be fittest for him: he is accommodated like a King, and served with such ceremonies as he had never seene before, and yet beheld them without saying any thing, and with an assured countenance. This done, the greatest Nobleman in the Dukes Court enters the chamber with the same reverence & honour to him as if he had been their Soveraigne Prince (Phillip with Princely delight beholds this play from a private place); divers of purpose petitioning him for pardons, which hee grants with such a continuance and gravity, as if he had a Crowne on his head all his life time.

Being risen late, and dinner time approaching, they asked him if he were pleased to have his tables covered. He likes that very well. The table is furnished, where he is set alone, and under a rich canopie; he eates with the same ceremony which was observed at the Dukes meales; he made good cheere, and chawed with all his teeth, but only drank with more moderation then he could have wisht, but the Majesty which he represented made him refraine. All taken away, he was entertained with new and pleasant things; they led him to walk about the great Chambers, Galleries, and Gardens of the Pallace (for all this merriment was played within the gates, they being shut only for recreation to the Duke and the principall of his Court): they shewed him all the richest and most pleasantest things therin, and talked to him thereof as if they had all beene his, which he heard with an attention and contentment beyond measure, not saying one word of his base condition, or declaring that they tooke him for another. They made him passe the afternoone in all kind of sports; musicke, dancing, and a Comedy, spent some part of the time. They talked to him of some State matters, whereunto he answered according to his skill, and like a right Twelfetide King.

Super time approaching, they aske this new created Prince if he would please to have the Lords & Ladies of his Court to sup and feast with him, whereat he seemed something unwilling, as if hee would not abase his dignity unto such familiarity: neverthelesse, counterfeiting humanity and affability, he made signes that he condiscended thereunto: he then towards night, was led with sound of Trumpets & Hoboyes into a faire hall, where long tables were set, which were presently covered with divers sorts of dainty meates, the Torches shined in every corner, and made a day in the midst of a night: the Gentlemen and Gentlewomen were set in fine order, and the Prince at the upper end in a higher seat. The service was magnificent, the musicke of voyces and instruments fed the eare, whilest mouthes found their food in the dishes. Never was the imaginary Duke at such a feast: carousses begin after the manner of the Country; the Prince is assaulted in all sides, as the Owle is assaulted by all the Birds, when he begins to soare. Not to seeme uncivill, he would doe the like to his good and faithfull subjects. They serve him with very strong wine, good Hipocras, which hee swallowed downe in great draughts, and frequently redoubled; so that charged with so many extraordinaryes, he yeelded to death's cousin german, sleep, which closed his eyes, stopt his eares, and made him loose the use of his reason and all his other senses.

Then the right Duke, who had put himselfe among the throng of his Officers to have the pleasure of this mummery, commanded that this sleeping man should be stript out of his brave cloathes, and cloathed againe in his old ragges, and so sleeping carried and layd in the same place where he was taken up the night before. This was presently done, and there did he snort all the night long, not taking any hurt either from the hardnesse of the stones or the night ayre, so well was his stomacke filled with good preservatives. Being awakened in the morning by some passenger, or it maye bee by some that the good Duke Philip had thereto appointed, ha! said he, my friends, what have you done? you have rob'd mee of a Kingdome, & have taken mee out of the sweetest & happiest dreame that ever man could have fallen into. Then, very well remembring all the particulars of what had passed the day before, he related unto them, from point to point, all that happened unto him, still thinking it assuredly to bee a dreame. Being returned home to his house, hee entertaines his wife, neighbours and friends, with this his dreame, as hee thought: the truth whereof being at last published by the mouthes of those Courtiers who had been present at this pleasant recreation, the good man could not beleeve it, thinking that for sport they had framed this history upon his dreame; but when Duke Philip, who would have the full contentment of this pleasant tricke, had shewed him the bed wherein he lay, the cloathes which he had worne, the persons who had served him, the Hall wherein he had eaten, the gardens and galleries wherein he had walked, hardly could hee be induced to beleeve what hee saw, imagining that all this was meere inchantment and illusion.

The Duke used some liberality towards him for to helpe him in the poverty of his family; and taking an occasion thereon to make an Oration unto his Courtiers concerning the vanity of this worlds honours, hee told them that all that ambitious persons seeke with so much industry is but smoake, and a meere dreame, and that they are strucken with that pleasant folly of the Athenian, who imagined that all the riches that arrived by shipping in the haven of Athens to be his, and that all the Marchants were but his factors: his friends getting him cured by a skilfull Physitian of the debility of his brain, in lieu of giving them thanks for this good office, he reviled them, saying that, whereas he was rich in conceit, they had by this cure made him poore and miserable in effect.

Harpaste, a foole that Senecaes wife kept, & whose pleasant imagination this grave Phylosopher doth largely relate, being growne blinde, could not perswade herselfe that she was so, but continually complained that the house wherein she dwelt was dark, that they would not open the windowes, and that they hindred her from setting light, to make her beleeve she could see nothing: hereupon this great Stoick makes this fine consideration that every vitious man is like unto this foole, who, although he be blind in his passion, yet thinks not himselfe to be so, casting all his defect on false surmises, whereby he seeks not only to have his sinne worthy of excuse and pardon, but even of praise: the same say the covetous, ambitious, and voluptuous persons in defence of their imperfections; but in fine (as the Psalmist saith) all that must passe awaye, and the images thereof come to nothing, as the dreame of him that awaketh from sleepe.

If a bucket of water be as truly water as all the sea, the difference only remaining in the quantity, not in the quality, why shall we not say, that our poore Brabander was a Soveraigne Prince for the space of fowre and twenty houres, being that he received all the honors and commodities thereof: how many Kings and Popes have not lasted longer, but have dyed on the very day of their Elections or Coronations? As for those other pompes which have lasted longer, what are they else but longer dreames? This vanity of worldly things is a great sting to a well composed soule, to helpe it forward towards the heavenly kingdome.

D

From Sir Richard Barckley's *A Discourse of the Felicitie of Man: or his Summum Bonum*, pp. 24-6

I remember a pretie experiment practised by the Emperour Charles the fift upon a drunkard.

As this Emperour on a time entered into Gaunt there lay a drunken fellow overthwart the streetes, as though he had bene dead, who least the horsemen should ride over him was d[r]awen out of the way by the legges, & culd by no means be wakened; which when the Emperour saw he caused him to be taken up and carried home to his pallace, and used as he had appointed. He was brought into a faire chamber hanged with costly arras, his clothes takē off, & laid in a stately bed meet for the Emperour him selfe. He continued in sleepe untill the next day almost noone. When he awaked and had lyen wōdring awhile to see him self in such a place and diverse brave gentlemen attending upon him, they took him out of the bed & apparelled him like a Prince, in verie costly garments & all this was done with verie great silence on everie side. When he was ready, there was a table set & furnished with verie daintie meats, and he set in a chaire to eate, attended upon with brave

Courtiers, & served as if the Emperour had bin present, the cupboord full of gold plate and diverse sortes of wines. When he saw such preparation made for him, he left any longer to wonder, and thought it not good to examine the matter any further, but tooke his fortune as it came and fell to his meate. His wayters with great reverence & dutie observed diligently his nods & becks, which were his signes, to call for that he lacked, for words he used none. As he thus sate in his maiestie eating and drinking, he tooke in his cups so freelie that he fel fast a sleepe againe as he sate in his chaire. His attendāts stripped him out of his fresh apparel, and arrayed him with his owne ragges againe, and carried him to the place where they found him, where he lay sleeping until the next day. After he was awakened, and fell into the companie of his acquaintance, being asked where he had bene, he answered that he had bene asleepe, and had the pleasantest dreame that ever he had in his life, and told them all that passed, thinking that it had been nothing but a dreame. The like peradventure would happen to the carowsers of these dayes, if they would clēse their minds frm this notorious vice of excessive quaffiing, evē to drunkennesse and somtimes to death, and consider that God hath made them a creature after his owne image, they would thinke or for shame wish that the time they had in that sort spent, had bin but a dreame.

APPENDIX III

THIS Appendix contains a reprint from *The Taming of the Shrew* in *The Old-Spelling Shakespeare* (Chatto & Windus, 1907) of a comparative list of characters in *The Taming of the Shrew*, *The Taming of a Shrew*, and Ariosto's *I Suppositi*, and a comparison of the plots of the three plays. Both the list and the analysis of the plots were the work of the late W. G. Boswell-Stone.

I have throughout assimilated the spelling of the names of the characters in *The Taming of a Shrew* to that adopted in my text, and I have omitted a few notes and references which bore only upon the Shakespearean play. To make the comparison of the plots easier I have added in square brackets the references to acts, scenes, and lines in the present edition of *A Shrew*, though Mr. Boswell-Stone's quotations are in the spelling of the quarto of 1594. His references to *The Shrew* are, of course, to his text in *The Old-Spelling Shakespeare*, and to *I Suppositi* to the text published in *Teatro Italiano Antico*, Vol. II., pp. 209-318 (Milan). Gascoigne's English version of Ariosto's comedy is now easily accessible in Prof. J. W. Cunliffe's edition of Gascoigne's *Works*, Vol. I. (Cambridge English Classics Series), and his edition of *Supposes* and *Jocasta* (Heath's Belles-Lettres Series).

A

A Comparative List of the Characters in *The Taming of the Shrew* and the parallel plays, *The Taming of a Shrew* and *I Suppositi*

The Taming of a Shrew	The Taming of the Shrew	I Suppositi.
Alfonso, *a merchant of* Athens.	Baptista, *a gentleman of* Padua.	Damonio, *a merchant of* Ferrara.
Jerobel, *Duke of* Cestus.	Vincentio, *a gentleman of* Pisa.	Filogono, *a merchant of* Catania.
Aurelius, *son to* Jerobel *and suitor to* Philema.	Lucentio, *son to* Vincentio, *and suitor to* Bianca.	Erostrato, *son to* Filogono, *and suitor to* Polinesta.
Ferando, *the* Shrew-tamer.	Petruchio, *the* Shrew-tamer.	
Polidor, *a student at* Athens, *friend to* Aurelius, *and suitor to* Emelia.	Hortensio, *a gentleman of* Padua, *friend to* Petruchio, *and suitor to* Bianca.	
	Gremio, *an old* "Pantalowne," *suitor to* Bianca.	Cleandro, *an old* Doctor of Laws, *suitor to* Polinesta.
Valeria, *servant to* Aurelius, *whom he personates.*	Tranio, *servant to* Lucentio, *whom he personates.*	Dulippo, *servant to* Erostrato, *whom he personates.*
Catapie, Polidor's *Boy.*	Biondello, Lucentio's *Boy.*	Caprino, Erostrato's *Boy.*
Sander, *servant to* Ferando.	Grumio, *servant to* Petruchio.	
Phylotus, *a merchant who personates* Jerobel.	*A* Pedant, *who personates* Vincentio.	*A* Sanese *who personates* Filogono.
A Tailor.	*A* Tailor.	
A Haberdasher.	*A* Haberdasher.	
Servingmen *to* Ferando.	Servingmen *to* Petruchio.	
Kate, *the* Shrew, Alfonso's *eldest daughter.*	Katherine, *the* Shrew, Baptista's *elder daughter.*	
Philema, Alfonso's *second daughter.*	Bianca, Baptista's *younger daughter.*	Polinesta, Damonio's *only daughter.*
Emelia, Alfonso's *third daughter.*	*A* Widow *who marries* Hortensio.	
Scene: Athens, *and* Ferando's country-house.	Scene: Padua, *and* Petruchio's country-house.	Scene: Ferrara.

B

Comparison of the Plots in *The Taming of the Shrew*, *The Taming of a Shrew*, and *I Suppositi*.[1]

The Induction to *The Shrew* is an enlarged version of that which precedes *A Shrew*. *A Shrew* has four short Interludes [I. i. 324-31; III. vi. 78-9 and IV. i. 1; IV. ii. 45-53; IV. ii. 126-33], between which the action of the external play is resumed. In the last Interlude Sly falls asleep again, whereupon the Lord bids his men [IV. i. 127-31]:

> . . . "go take him easily vp,
> And put him in his one apparel againe,
> And lay him in the place where we did find him,
> Iust vnderneath the alehouse side below,
> But see you wake him not in any case."

Day is dawning when [*Epilogue*] the tapster re-enters, awakes Sly, and advises him to go home, for fear of his wife's anger. Sly answers that he has dreamed how to tame a shrew, if need be. Wishing to hear the dream, the tapster proposes to accompany him to his home, and they leave the stage together. In *The Shrew* there is only one brief interlude (I. i. 238-43, p. 24), unlike its source both in phrase and matter, and Sly's adventure is then allowed to drop away entirely.

Act. I., sc. i.—The first scene of *A Shrew* [I. i. 1-99] is laid before Alfonso's house at Athens. Aurelius (Lucentio),

[1] The comparison with the two source-plays follows the order of Act and scene in *The Shrew*.

Polidor (Hortensio), and their servants Valeria (Tranio) and Catapie, enter. Polidor, a student at Athens, welcomes his friend Aurelius, son of Jerobel (Vincentio), Duke of Cestus. Aurelius has left Jerobel's court, to visit Polidor. Alfonso (Baptista)), an Athenian merchant, enters with his three daughters, Kate (the Shrew), Philema, and Emelia. Polidor and Aurelius stand apart, regarding them. Alfonso sends his daughters to the church, and goes himself to the quay. On their departure, Polidor tells Aurelius that he loves Emelia, but cannot become a suitor for her because Alfonso has sworn that Kate "first shall be espowsde." Aurelius says that he has fallen in love with Philema. Polidor then sends his boy Catapie to fetch Ferando (Petruchio), who is Kate's equal in wealth and person, and, being also "as blunt in speech as she is sharpe of toong," may, he hopes, venture to marry her. Aurelius determines to woo Philema in the character of a "Marchants sonne of Cestus"; his servant Valeria assuming, in the meanwhile, the name and dress of "the Duke of Cestus sonne." *I Suppositi* opens with a dialogue between Polinesta (Bianca), daughter of Damonio (Baptista), a merchant of Ferrara, and her nurse. Polinesta says that Erostrato (Lucentio), son of Filgono (Vincentio), a merchant of Catania, came to Ferrara to study law. On his arrival he met her in the high street, fell in love with her at once, and abandoning all thought of study, exchanged both clothes and name with his servant Dulippo, who had accompanied him from Catania. Thus disguised, Erostrato managed to enter Damonio's service. Dulippo, in the meanwhile, studied diligently (cp. *The Shrew*, I. i. 187). The similarity between the three plays is here close; the only difference being that in *I Suppositi* the master takes the servant's name. Cleandro (Gremio), a rich old doctor of laws, is a suitor for Polinesta's hand, and in order to mar his wooing, the sham Erostrato plays the part of a rival.

Act I., sc. ii.—In *A Shrew* [I. i. 100-29] the action proceeds. Catapie's errand is anticipated by the entrance of Ferando and Sander (Grumio), immediately after Aurelius has expressed his intention of exchanging characters with Valeria. Ferando announces to Polidor an already-formed resolve to woo Kate, her father having promised him 6000 crowns if he should succeed. He desires the two friends to "stand aside," whereupon he will make Alfonso bring Kate out of the house and leave her with him. Polidor and Aurelius then quit the stage, and Sander retires from view.

Act II., sc. i.—In *A Shrew* Ferando's wooing of Kate precedes her music-lesson. Left alone, Ferando [I. i. 130-40] summons Alfonso and desires him to bring forth Kate, and, after a brief absence, return in order to join their hands and fix the wedding-day. Alfonso calls Kate forth and departs, exhorting her to treat her wooer "as friendlie" as she can. Then follows a dialogue [I. i. 144-71] between Ferando and Kate, which is the original of *The Shrew*, II. i. 179-272. Alfonso, returning [I. i. 172-222], appoints the wedding-day, and retires with Kate. Ferando departs, after bidding Sander remain to inform Polidor of the approaching marriage, and of his temporary absence in the country. Catapie [I. i. 223-75] enters and asks Sander where Ferando is to be found. Before the question is answered, Polidor, Aurelius, and Valeria re-enter. Sander delivers his master's message, and goes out with Catapie. Valeria—"as erste we did devise" [I. i. 276], says Aurelius—taking his lute, goes to Alfonso's house, Alfonso having, as Polidor remarks [I. 279-81],

> "... spoke to me,
> To helpe him to some cunning Musition,
> To teach his eldest daughter on the lute."

In *The Shrew*, I. i. 95-7, Baptista makes a similar application to Hortensio[1] and Gremio. Polidor proposes [I. i. 286-95] that, whilst Kate is having her music-lesson, he and Aurelius should seize the opportunity of courting her sisters, who will then be able "to stele abrode" unhindered by her. Alfonso re-enters [I. i. 296], and thanks Polidor for sending such a skilful musician, who, he adds, is now about to give Kate a lesson. So, in *The Shrew*, II. i., Hortensio, after being presented to Baptista, is at once despatched to his pupil. Tranio makes himself known to Baptista. Polidor introduces Aurelius to Alfonso as "a wealthie Marchants sonne of Cestus" [I. i. 302]. The first scene of *A Shrew* now ends, all entering Alfonso's house.

No appreciable interval of time elapses, however, before Valeria enters with Kate [II. i. 1]. The music-lesson, of which Hortensio delivers a report, was witnessed by the spectators of *A Shrew*. Valeria wishes a false stop to be played over again, whereupon his pupil waxes wroth, offers to strike him with the lute, and then flinging it down, sweeps away. She had bidden Valeria beware [II. i. 29-31]

[1] The reader will remark that Hortensio's disappearance causes no surprise to Gremio and Tranio. Hortensio's purpose was to court Bianca, without Gremio's knowledge. See I. ii. 132, 133. But some excuse for his apparent absence should have been devised. In *A Shrew* Valeria is the musician, and Polidor (Hortensio) does not efface himself by a disguise.

. . . "least I cross your pate,
And make your musicke flie about your eares:
Ile make it and your foolish coxcombe meet";

and warned him to [II. i. 35-6]

. . . "come no more into this place,
Least that I clap your fiddle on your face."

The latter threat, and the advice she had previously offered him [II. i. 14-15]—

"Then make a night cap of your fiddles case,
To warme your head, and hide your filthie face!"

—perhaps suggested the ludicrous picture of Hortensio pilloried in his own lute. Gremio's taunt (*The Shrew*, II. i. 392-5) may be an echo of Cleandro's reply to a parasite named Pasifilo, on learning that Dulippo-Erostrato has undertaken to endow Polinesta with a marriage portion of 2000 ducats, the sum already promised by her aged suitor. Cleandro says (p. 222):

"Può Erostrato
Far dunque tale offerta, e entrare in obbligo
Alcuno, *cum sit filius familias?*"[1]

Act III., sc. i. bears no resemblance to any scene either in *A Shrew* or *I Suppositi*.

Act III., sc. ii.—The action of *A Shrew* continues. To Valeria soliloquizing on Kate's shrewishness, enter Aurelius, Polidor, Emelia, and Philema [II. i. 47]. On hearing the untoward result of the music-lesson, Aurelius orders Valeria

1 Can Erostrato make such an offer, and give a bond, seeing that he is a minor?

to go to his chamber, and entertain one who has come from Cestus "to daie" [II. i. 54]. This person is doubtless the merchant Phylotus, who is hereinafter to play the same part which belongs to the Pedant in *The Shrew* and to the Sanese in *I Suppositi*. Alfonso enters [II. i. 86], marvelling at Ferando's absence. Such is the rapidity of the action that the wedding day has already arrived.[1] Philema and Emelia are sent to Kate, who is engaged with her toilet. Like Baptista, Alfonso fears that[2] the bridegroom may have changed his mind. Like Tranio, Polidor endeavours to reassure the anxious father. Then enters Ferando [II. i. 108], "baselie attired," and we have the dialogue which forms the parallel of *The Shrew*, III. ii. 80-116. As he says, "And therefore take me thus or not at all" [II. i. 138], Kate appears, and answers his question—"shall we go to church"—by flatly refusing to marry "such a filthie slauish groome." Ferando addresses her in a strain of extravagant flattery which, presumably, appeases her wrath, for she says no more, and they set out for church, Alfonso and the rest following. Sander and Catapie now enter [II. ii. 1], and their talk fills the time during which the wedding is celebrated. The description of the marriage ceremony in *The Shrew*, III. ii. 142-76,

[1] "In the old Play of the *Taming of a Shrew* the whole story is knit up in the course of two days. In the first, Ferando = Petruchio woos Kate and fixes his marriage for 'next Sunday'; 'next Sunday' then becomes to-morrow, to-morrow becomes to-day, and to-day ends with the wedding night in Ferando's country house. All the rest of the Play is included in the second day."—P. A. Daniel's Time-Analysis of *The Shrew in New Sh. Soc. Trans.*, 1877-9, p. 169.

[2] The result of Hortensio's effacement is that Tranio answers for the honesty of Petruchio, with whom he has, at most, only two days' acquaintance. In *A Shrew*, Polidor (Hortensio) vouches for his old friend Ferando.

has no parallel in *A Shrew*. The wedding-party return [II. ii. 54], and Ferando insists on carrying off the bride, as Petruchio does in *The Shrew*, III. ii. 177-231. After Emelia's speech, "They're euen as well macht as I would wish" [II. i. 94], some speculation ensues. Philema doubts Ferando's ability to tame Kate. Aurelius questions the efficiency of Kate's "manhood." Polidor hesitatingly agrees with Philema. He proposes to visit the new-married pair within "this two daies." Alfonso then questions Aurelius [II. i. 110-14]:

> "What haue you sent to Cestus as you said,
> To certifie your father of your loue?
> For I would gladlie he would like of it;
> And if he be the man you tell to me,
> I guess he is a Marchant of great wealth."

Aurelius replies that he expects his father to visit Athens "within this weeke at most." This preparation for the sham-father part of the plot—of which we have already had a hint—should be compared with the colloquy between Lucentio and Tranio, in *The Shrew*, III. ii. 121-41. The scene now closes, all, as in *The Shrew*, leaving the stage to partake of the wedding dinner.

Act IV., sc. i.—The corresponding scene in *A Shrew* [III. i.] is laid at Ferando's house.

Act IV., sc. ii.—About half of this scene in *The Shrew* (ll. 1-52) is original. Next comes the jesting about Petruchio's shrew-taming school, which is taken almost *verbatim* from *A Shrew*. For the rest of the scene *I Suppositi* is the chief source, *A Shrew* [III. ii. 22-30] having here but slight resemblance to the Shakespearian play. On the opening of the Second Act of *I Suppositi*, Dulippo relates to Erostrato how Damonio had been persuaded to wait fifteen days before giving his daughter in marriage; within which time Filogono—whom Damonio required to subscribe Erostrato's bond—was expected at Ferrara.

As Dulippo was issuing from Ferrara, he saw (p. 234)

> . . . "un gentil uom scender da l'argine,
> Uomo attempato, il quale ha assai buon' aria."[1]
>
> (Cp. *The Shrew*, IV. ii. 60-2.)

Dulippo asked him whence he came and whither he was going. The traveller replied that he came from Padua, having previously visited Venice, and was now returning to his native city, Siena. Hereupon Dulippo affected great surprise; and, when asked the reason, answered that some ambassadors to the King of Naples, sent by Ercole II., Duke of Ferrara, and returning with costly presents from the King to the Duke, had been stayed by the custom-house officers of Siena, and obliged to pay duty on the royal gifts as though they had been merchants' wares. To Ercole's complaint of this discourtesy the Republic of Siena made such an insolent response that the Duke, in great wrath, swore upon the host that all the Sanesi found in his dominions should be driven away with disgrace: further, that innkeepers who received them and did not give immediate notice of their arrival, should incur a heavy penalty. Upon hearing this, the traveller was about to ride off, but, by Dulippo's advice, consented instead to pass for the merchant (*mercatante*, cp. *The Shrew*, IV. ii. 63) Filogono of Catania, and lodge in his reputed son's house. Dulippo

[1] A gentleman coming down from the embankment, an elderly man, of passably good mien. (The Po is embanked at Ferrara.)

trusted, ere the Sanese discovered how he had been duped, to win his good-will by politeness and hospitality, and thus engage him to join in the plot by giving security, in Filogono's name, for two or three thousand ducats, or more. At the close of this explanation the Sanese, whom Dulippo has left at an inn until Erostrato should sanction the scheme, enters with a servant. After some talk, Dulippo, the Sanese, and the servant enter the sham-Erostrato's house. In the corresponding scene of *A Shrew* [III. ii.] Aurelius and Valeria enter, and the former, after telling Valeria—apparently for the first time—of his love for Philema, says that he hopes to marry her [III. ii. 13-6]:

> "If that the marchant which thou toldst me of
> Will (as he sayd) go to Alfonsos house,
> And say he is my father, and there with all
> Pas ouer certain deedes of land to me."

Aurelius, wishing to see Phylotus, goes out to meet him conducted by Valeria.

Act IV. sc. iii.—In *A Shrew*—the sole source of this scene—the shrew-taming action is interrupted [after III. iii.], and a parallel scene [III. iv.] to *The Shrew*, IV. iv. precedes that [III. v.] in which Ferando undertakes to regulate Kate's wardrobe, and insists on her accepting his reckoning of time.

Act IV. sc. iv.—The resemblance to *A Shrew* [III. iv.] in this scene does not extend beyond l. 73. Aurelius, Valeria and Phylotus enter, on their way to Alfonso's house. Having cautioned Phylotus to remember his lesson,[1] Aurelius summons Alfonso. Alfonso comes to his door,

1 "For you doo very much resemble him" [III. iv. 5], says Aurelius. Cp. *The Shrew* IV. ii. 100.

and is introduced by Aurelius to Phylotus. Phylotus, responding to Alfonso's welcome, says that he is aware of Aurelius's choice, which he does not 'mislike.' He offers to settle £300 a year on his son, and pay down 1000 ingots of pure gold, and 2000 bars of silver plate, confirming these promises "in writing straight." Alfonso commends Phylotus's fatherly liberality, consents to the match, and engages to enlarge his daughter's dowry. Alfonso is then presented by Aurelius to Valeria, who personates, as before arranged, the Duke of Cestus's son. Phylotus wishes the marriage settlements to be drawn up in Valeria's presence, and, at Alfonso's invitation, Valeria accompanies them to Alfonso's house, where the business is to be transacted. The scene [III. v.] of *A Shrew*, which is the source of *The Shrew*, IV. iii. 59-191, ends with Ferando's declaration to Kate: "Ile haue you say as I doo ere you go." To this succeeds a scene [III. vi.] which has no parallel in *The Shrew*. The wedding day of Kate's sisters has come. Polidor, Emelia, Aurelius and Philema enter, and after an interchange of high-flown compliments depart for the church, where Alfonso and "the reste" are awaiting them.

Act IV. sc. v.—While Kate's sisters are being married, she and Ferando [IV. i.] are somewhere on the road to Athens. Kate's speech—ending with a hope that Athens may not be exposed to the unveiled lustre of his "louely face"—convinces the Duke of Cestus that she is as mad as her husband; and, "for feare of harme," he rides on ahead. Ferando praises Kate for her obedience, and they follow the Duke, intending to "perswade him to his shape againe" [IV. i. 55].

Act V. sc. i.—*I Suppositi* has furnished the chief material for this scene of *The Shrew*. Dulippo, having obtained a sham-father for his master Erostrato, was very anxious to find the parasite Pasifilo whom he proposed sending to Damonio, to announce Filogono's arrival and willingness to guarantee the requisite marriage portion. Hearing that Pasifilo had been seen outside the gate of S. Paolo, Dulippo went to seek him. At the place where the ships were unloaded, a boat came ashore in which he saw Lizio his fellow-servant, and Filogono. He immediately fled in order to warn Erostrato, whom he expects to find in Damonio's house. Waiting outside the house for Erostrato, he espies Filogono and Lizio approaching, and is obliged to take to his heels. Filogono and Lizio are accompanied by a Ferrarese, their host, who has offered to show them the sham Erostrato's house. At this point the parallel with *The Shrew*, V. i. 7-69, begins. On reaching the house the Ferrarese knocks without result, whereupon Lizio hammers at the door. Dalio, the sham Erostrato's cook, looks out from a window. Filogono asks for Erostrato, and, being told that he is not at home, demands to be admitted. Dalio answers that Filogono cannot be received in the house; another stranger has taken all the spare room. On further enquiry, Filogono learns that this stranger is Filogono of Catania, Erostrato's father. Asked when the stranger arrived Dalio replies that he alighted at the Angel ("*all' Angelo*") two hours or more ago, and was brought to the house by Erostrato. Filogono wishes to see the stranger, and Dalio retires from the window to summon him. The Sanese comes to the door. In answer to Filogono's enquiries he asserts himself to be Filogono, a merchant of Catania, and Erostrato's father. Filogono rates the Sanese. Dalio threatens Filogono, and invites the Sanese to re-enter the house. The

Ferrarese descries the sham Erostrato, and brings him face to face with Filogono. Both Filogono and Lizio recognize Dulippo. Dulippo denies having ever seen Filogono. He says that every one in Ferrara knows him as Erostrato, and appeals to the Ferrarese, who confirms the statement. Lizio suspects that the Ferrarese and Dulippo are leagued to cheat Filogono. Declining to listen any longer to such nonsense, Dulippo moves to enter his house. Filogono reviles Dulippo, and says (p. 287):

> . . . "ch' hai tu di Erostrato
> Fatto, assassino, poichè 'l suo nome occupi?" [1]

Cp. *The Shrew*, V. i. 69. Dulippo restrains Dalio's violence, and withdraws with him into the house. Guided by the Ferrarese, Filogono departs to obtain legal advice from an advocate.[2] Thus in *I Suppositi* the impostors are able to hold their own, but in *A Shrew*, as in *The Shrew*, the unwinding of the plot is quickly brought about. With *The Shrew*, V. i. 87-113, *A Shrew* [IV. ii.] must be compared, l. 94 excepted, where Lucentio confesses to Baptista that he has married Bianca

> "While counterfeit *supposes* bleer'd thine eine."

Here "supposes" is evidently applied to those who assume the character and appearance of other persons, whom they are supposed to be; *i.e. suppositi*, or "supposes" according to Gascoigne's title. His daughter's marriage being over,

[1] What have you done with Erostrato, murderer, since you usurp his name?

[2] Filogono is introduced to Cleandro (Gremio). The *dénouement* of *I Suppositi* is delayed in order that Dulippo-Erostrato may prove to be Cleandro's son, who had been lost when a child.

Alfonso invites the wedding-party to his house "to see what cheere we haue." He wonders at the absence of Ferando and Kate. Phylotus promises Alfonso ship-loads of costly gifts,—amongst which he enumerates "Arras counter poines," cp. *The Shrew*, II. i. 343,—and Valeria undertakes, in still more generous sort, to enrich his friend Polidor's father-in-law. The Duke of Cestus, entering unobserved, overhears Valeria. A few speeches in *The Shrew* bear some resemblance to what follows. Says the Duke to Valeria [IV. ii. 31-2]:

"Are you become the Duke of Cestus son,
And reuels with my treasure in the towne?

(Cp. V. i. 54, 55)

Val. Sounes! it is the Duke, what shall I doo?

(Cp. V. i. 34, 35)

Duke. Her's no villaine! he will not know me now.
[*To Phi.*] But what say you? have you not forgot me too?

(Cp. V. i. 38)

Aur. Pardon me, father! humblie on my knees,

(Cp. V. i. 89, and stage-direction in F.)

I do intreat your grace to heare me speake!"

The Duke, however, orders [IV. ii. 43-4] that Phylotus and Valeria be sent to prison. They like Tranio and the Pedant, run away. Cp. the second F. stage-direction at V. i. 89. The Duke storms at Aurelius and Valeria, in "Ercles vein." Aurelius and Philema offer their lives to appease his wrath. Their submission, and the entreaties of Polidor and Emelia, prevail, and he acknowledges the marriage. Refusing

Alfonso's invitation to the wedding banquet, and promising to revisit him in state "ere't be long," Jerobel departs, attended to his ship by Aurelius. Alfonso and the rest then leave the stage.

ACT V., SC. II.—This scene is wholly derived from *A Shrew* [V. i.]. Some time after Jerobel's exit, Ferando and Kate reached Athens. Supper is now over, and Ferando proves himself to be a complete Shrew-tamer.

ALEXANDER MORING LIMITED
THE DE LA MORE PRESS
32 GEORGE ST. HANOVER SQ.
LONDON ENGLAND